Love Traditions
in
Vidyapati & British Poets

Dr. Madan Mohan Jha

© **Madan Mohan Jha 2020**

All rights reserved

All rights reserved by author. No part of this publication may be reproduced, stored in a retrieval system or transmitted in any form or by any means, electronic, mechanical, photocopying, recording or otherwise, without the prior permission of the author.

Although every precaution has been taken to verify the accuracy of the information contained herein, the author and publisher assume no responsibility for any errors or omissions. No liability is assumed for damages that may result from the use of information contained within.

First Published in July 2020

ISBN: 978-81-946726-8-5

Price: INR 300/-

BLUEROSE PUBLISHERS

www.bluerosepublishers.com
info@bluerosepublishers.com
+91 8882 898 898

Cover Design:
Sanya Rastogi

Typographic Design:
Namrata Saini

Distributed by: BlueRose, Amazon, Flipkart, Shopclues

Contents

Acknowledgement .... *v*
Preface .... *vii*

Chapter One- Introduction 1
Chapter Two- The love tradition an observation 25
Chapter Three- Style and Features 49
Chapter Four- Vidyapati and British Poets 71
Chapter Five- Forms of Love 93
Chapter Six- Fascination and Fantasy 115
Chapter Seven- Conclusion 142
Bibliography 162

Acknowledgement

I am very thankful to the almighty whose blessings are very necessary for success in life. The present work is the outcome of five years of rigorous work of not only mine but of different people. I cannot forget their help and support which always inspired me to work hard and achieve this zenith . First of all I would like to start this acknowledgement by expressing my gratitude towards my supervisor Dr. A. K. Bachchan, Professor, University Department of English, Lalit Narayan Mithila University, who always guided me to finish this research work. He is not only my supervisor but a source of inspiration and without him it was impossible to complete this task. I am feeling blessed in showing my gratitude towards prof. A. K Jha, former head of the English Department, Lalit Narayan Mithila University, Darbhanga, Bihar , who has suggested me this topic and also motivated me to sharpen my intellectuality. I would also like to mention Dr. Aroonima Sinha, Professor and Head, University Department of English, Lalit Narayan Mithila University, Dr. Punita Jha, Professor, University Department of English, Lalit Narayan Mithila University, Dr. Pratibha Gupta,Associate Professor, University Department of English, Lalit Narayan Mithila University, Dr. Pushpa Jha, Dr. Kulanand Yadav, Controller of Examinations, Lalit Narayan Mithila University, Dr. N.K. Yadav, Deputy Controller of Examinations, Lalit Narayan Mithila

University who have contributed a lot in completing this research work. Apart from these people I would like to thank my wife Prity Kumari who always stood for me even in my weaker days. How can I forget my grandfather late Ramanand Jha who was always a source of inspiration for me. There were several occasions when I felt that this research work is very tough then I was motivated by my father Amar Kant Jha so I mention a special thanks to him. I am indebted to my friends Rakesh Kumar, Kailash Chandra Jha, Parmendra Mishra, Chandan Jha, Sunil Kumar Sharda, Nagmani Alok, Raman Kumar Rajesh, Mithilesh Manjhi, Mr.Sangeet Ranjan Natwar, Head, Department of English, J.N. College, Nehra, Amit Kumar and Mukesh Mahato. They gave me different ideas which helped me in making this work interesting. Apart from all of them I would like to mention the name of my brothers Man Mohan Jha and Hari Mohan Jha and mother Smt. Ramila Jha who were always there when I needed them the most. The non teaching staff of the Department of English Lalit Narayan Mithila University Ashok Gupta, is also worth mentioning here. He was also very supportive and cooperative. My sister in laws Preeti Jha and Chandra Kumari assisted me a lot so I sincerely present thanks to them.

(MADAN MOHAN JHA)

Preface

Vidyapati has always been a very special poet for me. Since my childhood I am accustomed to listening to his songs and poems. My mother tongue is Maithili and the whole canon of Maithili Literature is incomplete without the songs and poems of Vidyapati. I remember once I was in Delhi and suddenly somewhere I heard a song of Vidyapati and my senses started to give response. I was feeling that I am at my home town and then I decided that if given a chance I will try to explore more about this poet. I have felt immense pleasure while completing this research work and it is kind of honor to work upon such a blessed poet. He belongs to the age of Chaucer but in his poems and songs we can feel that almost all of his creations are ageless. There is a universal appeal of love and devotion in his poems. I have divided my thesis into seven chapters. In **Chapter One**, which is the *Introduction*, the life and times of Vidyapati, the influences that developed his artistic mind has been explored. His writings are the result of experience and keen observation and acute understanding of human nature. **The Second chapter** entitled *The love tradition an observation* covers the horizons of love from its starting. **The Third chapter** is based entirely on the stylistic features of love poems written by Vidyapati and few British poets. The chapter entitled *style and features* covers mainly Vidyapati and Romantic poets like John Keats, Byron, Shelley, Wordsworth,

Coleridge and others. There is also a comparative study of the stylistic features of John Donne and Vidyapati. **The Fourth chapter** is entitled Vidyapati and British poets and it covers the love tradition of Vidyapati and British Poets. **The Fifth chapter** is entitled, *Forms of Love* and it encompasses the Platonic, metaphysical and few other concept of love. **The Sixth Chapter** is based on fascination and fantasy. The fascination of Vidyapati has been compared to some British Poets and the role of fantasy has also been discussed. In the **Seventh Chapter,** which is the **Conclusion,** I have tried to show Vidyapati as a poet who implied classic and modern themes, modeled on his own religious beliefs, through allegory and symbols. I have also tried to focus on his use of lyrical notes that remained fairly consistent from devotional poems to love poems and which is exclusive to the time period of Vidyapati. This research work is an attempt to show that Vidyapati is far ahead of his time as well as his contemporaries.

Chapter One

Introduction

Vidyapati is a renowned Maithili poet as well as a Sanskrit writer. He was born in 1352 in Bisfi, a village situated in Madhubani district of Bihar. He was a well known poet of his time who was very far ahead of his contemporaries. His poetry was very influential and it was circulated in Maithili, Abahatta and Sanskrit. His poetry has also influenced languages like Hindustani, Nepali along with some other dialects which later got included in Maithili and Bengali. He has contributed a lot in formulating these languages so he is like Chaucer of England. Vidyapati is a kind of writer who is best known for his love poems and prayer songs. Sometimes he is also referred as kokil in Maithili literature. His father's name was Ganpati Thakur and it is believed that he has given the name Vidyapati to his son. His father was also a man of society who stood always for the common cause of the society. In books and several research papers the name of his father has been mentioned very less as there is very little information about him. In the poetry section of

Maithili Literature it has been mentioned that Vidyapati has written his poems on different subjects and Lord Siva is his inspiration. He has also written on topics like law, geography, history and ethics. We are concerned more about his poems which deal with human values governing emotion and love. His love poems are very famous and his poem on Radha and Krishna has influenced several writers of Mithila as well as Bengal. Vidyapati has also been acclaimed by several Bengali writers that he was a Bengali writer. The reason behind it is the similarities in language between Maithili and Bengali. The influence was so strong that the poems on Radha and Krishna were celebrated in different regions of Mithila as well as Bengal. The impact of such culture gave rise to a different language known as Brajabuli. It was a language which was neither Maithili nor Bengali but it was the mixture of the two. This language came into prominence in sixteenth century which was basically Maithili but modified with Bengali intonation. The Bengali poets of medieval history like Gobindadas Kabiraj, Narrotam Das, Balaram das and several others wrote in Brajabuli. Witers like Bankim Chandra Chatterjee and Rabindra Nath Tagore also wrote in this language. So, it shows that it was the new language of Indian renaissance. The poems of Vidyapati have not only inspired Bengali writers but through these writers it also reached to Odisha. Poets like Champati Ray, Ramananda and king Pratap Malla Dev were highly motivated and inspired by the poems of Vidyapati. In his poems we can trace some instances of kalidasa as well as Jaidev. The biography of Vidyapati can be traced from his creation *Kirtilata* where we can find Lakshman Samvat 252. It says that Vidyapati was in touch with different dynasties of Oinwar which is today's area of Pusa, Samastipur.

According to Kirtilata, Alsan killed Ganeshwar who was the ruler of Mithila. At that time, Vidyapati's father Pandit Ganpati Thakur was associated with the courtly culture of that ruler. He often visited his court to give him religious as well as political guidance. Vidyapati also used to visit the court in his childhood with his father. During those periods, he was ten or twelve years old. Maharaj Shiv Singh was the great ruler of same dynasty who always favoured Vidyapati as a friend as well as a poet. Vidyapati was two years older than Shiv Singh and thus they both knew each other well. Vidyapati has written several poems and dedicated it to Maharaj Shiv Singh and his favorite queen Lakhima Devi. In Kirtilata, the poet writes the reason that he favours the language of Abahatta because everybody does not like Sanskrit, and Prakrit was not understood by all so the poet decided to write in the local language so that it can be understood by all the segments of the society. There were several rulers who praised Vidyapati but Shiv Singh was the greatest admirer of the poet. He was a true patriot, virtuous and accomplished man. The sultans of Delhi used to captivate such rulers who were young, virtuous and accomplished. Even Prince Shiv Singh was captivated by the Sultan of Delhi. Vidyapati went to Delhi so that he can persuade the sultan of Delhi to grant freedom to his friend. In the court of the Sultan Vidyapati said that he was a poet and he could describe things lively without actually seeing them properly. The Sultan was moved greatly and he tried to take a test of Vidyapati. He asked the poet to prove his worth and it resulted into a beautiful poetry. The sultan was greatly moved by the poetry of Vidyapati and as a reward he granted freedom and respect to Shiv Singh. Apart from these things when we look into the dynamics of his poetry we will find that there are a lot of poetic devices which has been used by the poet. After reading his poetry we can also find a pleasure as well as a strange power to understand the human bond of love and affection. He was brave enough to write into Maithili in the region when Islam was spreading quickly into the territory of Mithila. We can also feel immense similarities between the rasas evoked by Kalidasa as well as Vidyapati. In describing the beauty of a woman, Vidyapati has used such beautiful words which can evoke a mild passion in the heart of the reader. His poems are the ornaments and it can be felt only by the deep rooted meanings of his poetry. It is not easy to understand his poetry however he never used difficult words or diction in his poem. Kalidasa has written about Shakuntala that this lady is the symbol of beauty. She has been compared to the beautiful flowers and such a comparison distinguishes Kalidasa from other poets. We will be surprised to find that Vidyapati too has written about the beauty of Shakuntala and he goes one step further and says that her beauty is like moon and her face has been washed by the droplets of divinity. Even in that period Vidyapati can compose such a beautiful poetry is remarkable. During the age of Petrarch there were similar objects which were subjectified. It is very interesting to see that Petrarch too was born in the same century and there is a kind of similarity between some of the subjects of Vidyapati as well as Petrarch. If we see the writing pattern of Petrarch, we can notice that he is rightly acknowledged as a model for Italian style. He is often called as the father of humanism. His sonnets are world famous. In one of his works *Secretum meum*, he has tried to establish a relationship between artist and God. Artist in form of secular achievements and the varieties still to work upon. He says that God has gifted human beings a special intellect and it became the spirit of Renaissance. Petrarch valued literature and ancient history the most and he also struggled to establish a relationship between contemplative and active life. If we read and analyze Petrarchan sonnets, we can see that almost all the sonnets have flexible rhyme scheme. There is a beautiful relationship between the lover and the beloved. This kind of relationship is similar to the relationship between a master and a slave. The beloved is treated as a guiding star and the lover tries to follow her. In the poems of Vidyapati, we can also trace that the beloved has been referred as the most beautiful lady in the life of the lover. Her body parts have been ornamented by the words of the poet. The poet is a kind of person who takes inspirations from tradition and culture. This is one of the reasons that in the poems of Vidyapati we can also find some deep rooted folk values. This can be seen in the love poems attributed to Radha and Krishna. It is not only about Radha and Lord Krishna but it encompasses entire human kind. It reflects a bond between a lover and his beloved. This bond is not new but its beginning is the beginning of the human kind. It is known to the world that Vidyapati was a kind of poet who has written numerous poems on different Rasas. He has seen the real form of beauty and valour mixed together. There is nothing mystic in his writings yet his poems are not easy to understand. They are neither too tough but there is the kind of poetic genius in his writings which has been admired by different poets of not only his own age but of the current age also. Thus there is a kind of universality in his poems. What Shakespeare or Donne has written in their age has been written very earlier by this poet. It can be merely an exaggeration but it cannot be denied totally. The present research work is an attempt to encompass all the horizons of his poetry. The poetic beauty of this poet can be seen in his attempt to write in an age when Sanskrit language was most prominent in the entire region of Mithila. It was an age when Islamic culture flourished at height. There are numerous instances which hint that during this age temples were demolished. Vidyapati was a brave poet that is why, he chose Maithili as his language of poetry. As a poet he always emphasized upon to bring forward the beautiful life of human beings. John Milton later has written much on this topic that human beings were the most beautiful and intelligent creation of god. This instance can be seen in Vidyapati. He wrote for betterment of human understanding. He valued human beauty the most and he was a kind of writer for whom beauty always appealed the most. His masterpieces of writings are vivid examples to reflect such ideologies. Understanding his poetry has always been a very tough task. We need to understand different Rasa theories to understand his poetry. Vidyapati has explored almost all the basic human sentiments in his poems. Thus, we can say that he is able to invoke all the Rasas in different form and features. There are eight forms of Rasas and we can see all the forms in his poems. He has not only used these Rasas but he stands as a master in writing such kind of Poems. He is predominantly known best for Sringara-rasa poems. The Sambhog Sringara is the form of Sringara Rasa where a lover is enamored of the charms of the beloved at the very first sight. This kind of poetry has been termed often erotic but it is the beauty of the poetry which invokes most pure form of love and emotion. In different poems attributed to Radha and Krishna, we can see the fragrance of such kind of feelings which is serene. There are several beautiful lines which creates a kind of drama in the mind of readers and they are transported to the dialects of Bharta who said while narrating the origin of Natyasastra that-

> "Brahma meditated in solitude and finally decided to compose a fifth Veda incorporating all the arts and sciences, and enlightening too. This he did by taking words from Rigveda, music from Samveda, movements and make-up from Yajurveda, and emotional acting from Atharvanaveda."[1]

The above quotes can also be applied to Vidyapati. His poems invoke a similar sense of divinity and purity. His poems are not simply poems but it seems that he has poured his heart in his poetry. It is not personal but it can be applied anywhere. Thus there is a kind of universality of theme in his poems. Coming back to Sambhog Sringara, it is interesting to see that a lover watches his beloved as a unique creation of Brahma. Now comparing this to the concept of Platonic love, the concept of Wikipedia is worth mentioning here-

> "Platonic love is examined in Plato's dialogue, the Symposium, which has as its topic the subject of love or Eros generally. It explains the possibilities of how the feeling of love began and how it has evolved— both sexually and non-sexually. Of particular importance is the speech of Socrates, relating the idea of platonic love as attributed to the prophetess Diotima, which presents it as a means of ascent to contemplation of the divine. For Diotima, and for Plato generally, the most correct use of love of human beings is to direct one's mind to love of divinity. In short, with genuine platonic love, the beautiful or

lovely other person inspires the mind and the soul and directs one's attention to spiritual things. Socrates, in Plato's "Symposium", explained two types of love or Eros—Vulgar Eros or earthly love and Divine Eros or divine love. Vulgar Eros is nothing but mere material attraction towards a beautiful body for physical pleasure and reproduction. Divine Eros begins the journey from physical attraction i.e. attraction towards beautiful form or body but transcends gradually to love for Supreme Beauty. This concept of Divine Eros is later transformed into the term Platonic love."[2]

Now analyzing this form of Platonic love we can see that it starts from mind and enters the soul. It is a kind of inspiration both for the lover as well as the beloved. So in Vidyapati we can see similar kind of love which starts mind and then enters into soul. Thus, there is a kind of transportation from physical world to the world of serenity. This is purity of body and soul and there is nothing obscene in it. This understanding of the divinity of love can be seen mostly in Elizabethan poets like Philip Sidney and Edmund Spencer. *Astrophel and Stella* is a sonnet sequence written by Philip Sidney and here we can find poems of different emotions. The literal meaning of the title is star lover and star. Astrophel is the star lover and Stella is his star. The beloved is like a guiding star for the lover. The courtly culture which flourished during the Elizabethan period marked such beautiful poems which always inspired the forthcoming poets. There are few beautiful lines which are capable of evoking feelings inside the heart of readers. These lines are useful to be mentioned here-

"Loving in truth, and fain in verse my love to show,
That she (dear She) might take some pleasure of my pain:
Pleasure might cause her read, reading might make her know,
Knowledge might pity win, and pity grace obtain,
I sought fit words to paint the blackest face of woe,
Studying inventions fine, her wits to entertain:
Oft turning others' leaves, to see if thence would flow
Some fresh and fruitful showers upon my sun-burned brain.
But words came halting forth, wanting Invention's stay,
Invention, Nature's child, fled step-dame Study's blows,
And others' feet still seemed but strangers in my way.
Thus great with child to speak, and helpless in my throes,
Biting my truant pen, beating myself for spite,
'Fool' said my Muse to me, 'look in thy heart and write.'"[3]

The second line of the above quoted poem clearly reflects that the lover is expecting that his beloved might extract some pleasure of his pain. This pain can be the root cause of pity which might lead to grace. Elizabethan poets were inspired by the Petrarchan Sonnets which gave them the idea to write more about the complex topics like love. We can find such themes of love in Vidyapati. It is doubtless to say that he was very far ahead of his time. Kalidasa the great poet of Sanskrit has written about the beauty of Shakuntala that God has created her with hands of delicacy. She is so soft and serene that beauty might itself feel shy on its serenity. Vidyapati has gone beyond this description and has written on the same topic, that is, beauty of Shakuntala. He has described her saying that her face has been created by the twinkling of the stars and the moon. When we analyze such beautiful images created by writers like Kalidasa and Vidyapati, we can find that Sringara-Rasa is at its height. Now coming to the Vipralambha Sringara, first of all we should understand about this term Vipralambha. It is a kind of love which is evoked in separation. Several philosophers have said that the intensity of love can be measured in separation. There is no scale to measure love yet separation acts like a tool which can make a lover or a beloved sick enough to dive in life and feel lifeless. In the writings of Vidyapati, we can see the conditions of a lover and a beloved when they separate from each other. This condition can be termed as love sick condition. Kalidasa has also written much on such conditions of life which we call Vipralambha Sringara. There are several comparisons between Vidyapati and Kalidasa. It is needless to say that both are the greatest writers of their time, yet Vidyapati cannot attain the poetic beauty of kalidasa. Opinions may vary from person to person yet several scholars agree that Kalidasa was a much refined poet. Vipralambha is a more frequent rasa of Sringara Rasa and it has been used vividly by Kalidasa and Vidyapati. We can notice that the theme of Meghdutam written by kalidasa is Vipralambha Sringara. In Abhijnanasakuntalam, the actual union of Shakuntala and Dushyanata has been written in detail but we can see that most of the time Dushyanta is in a love sick condition. This condition of love sickness is heightened when Dushyanta sees the ring. Now he remembers the time he has spent with Shakuntala. In separation, he feels sick and the chamberlain describes his exact condition. This condition of love can be seen frequently in *Virah Vedna* poems of Vidyapati. The opening lines of his poems has become celebrated songs of not only Maithili speaking people but it has been translated in so many languages. The lover is named Madhav which is also a name of Lord Krishna. The opening line of the poem conveys that Madhav has gone to a far flung area and the beloved is trying to know about his condition. She curses her own destiny that she is away from him and there is nobody who can tell her about the well wishing of her lover. The poem is lovely and it appeals directly to the heart of the readers. The poem has a theme that separation is not bearable both for the lover as well as the beloved. The lady protagonist or the beloved conveys her message to the lover through her friend that if the lover even thinks to go to a foreign land leaving the beloved alone then she is no longer going to live. She will die as she cannot live without him. Thus, we can see that whatever be the reasons the beloved cannot live without the lover. There are several instances that a lover goes to a foreign land to earn his bread and butter. There must be some problems, that is why, he is unable to take his beloved along with him. These problems or reasons cannot satisfy the questions of the beloved. She urges the lover to take her with him but he goes alone. This condition of the lover as well as the beloved becomes so emotional that even the lines of the poem reflect their agony and pain. It is needless to say that such kind of love can be seen everywhere and that is it has been said that love is not simply unification of the lover and the beloved but it can be separation also. Thus, there is a continuous fight between reason and passion. The heart says something whereas the mind says something else. Such a kind of difference between reason and passion can also be seen in several British poets. In *Astrophel and Stella* we can see another kind of duality between the mind and the heart. Throughout the poem, we can notice the anguish of Astrophel. It seems that the lover Astrophel is struck between his love for Stella and his rational mind. The mind says that Stella is married and he cannot win her love but his heart wants to win her heart at any cost. He loves her deeply and cannot think to leave her. He knows and he is aware of the fact that his love for Stella is irrational and foolish but still he longs for her. The whole sequence of the poem is full of dialogues between passion and reason. Although, Astrophel understands at last that reason is going to win but it is his inability that he cannot forget his love. Here, we can trace that it has been inspired by the love poetry of Petrarch. The description of Laura by Petrarch in his poems is closely copied in Astrophel and Stella. Thus we can see that there can be various ways to express one's gratitude and love. The beloved has always been looked with respect by the lover not only in the Modern age, but almost, in every era. The poetic sketch of love is not an easy task to understand but poets are God gifted and they can create sense even in the trance state of their mind. In the continuous fight between reason and passion, mind and heart there are different results at different times. It creates a sense of drama which looks very realistic. It is the love and devotion which has changed the history of not only our country but of the entire world. When pagan temples were being demolished in Rome by Early Christians then the Roman senator Symmachus remarked that there cannot be one road to the heart of so great a mystery. These words automatically came to mind while writing the introductory part of this present Research work because poems of Vidyapati are not so easy to understand. These poems have several interpretations and we will not be wrong if we say them collectively a multifaceted work. The great modern poet and scholar T.S.Eliot has identified two important characteristics of a classic: The maturity of idiom and maturity of manners. In the whole tradition of the Western literary circles, he could be satisfied by just a single work which stands on his expectations Virgil's Aeneid. Even the great writers like Homer and Shakespeare were thus denied of their greatness as classical writers. Frank Kermode has found that the definition of a classic given by T.S.Eliot sounds imperialistic and thus he gave another definition which is more liberal. He has emphasized on the fact that patience is the precursor of a classic. It reflects the change of nature and subject with the change of time. This change travels faster from one culture to another culture. The beauty of a classical poem or text cannot be faded either by time or space. By saying all these things let us not be confused that Vidyapati was a classical poet. We also cannot deny that there were instances of classicism in his writings. His subject of writing often varies with time and space. Like the age of Shakespeare in England and Aeschylus in Greece the age of Vidyapati witnessed a refined blooming of Renaissance spirit. Either the music or the dance everything was well balanced and even the lyrics was exalted. Vidyapati has raised the standard of Renaissance spirit at its greatest height in such a way that it found itself expressing throughout the territory of not only Mithila but it even crossed the boundary of Tirhut. The greatness of the poet lies in the fact that he represented various cultures and languages and that is why we can say that he has naturalized himself with various traditions and cultures. It is interesting to see that seven cities claimed that Homer belonged to them as it was his birthplace. No other poet or writer has been given such a respect but Vidyapati was also acclaimed as a poet of three different languages and people of three different languages followed him blindly. These three different languages are Maithili, Hindi and Bengali. Grierson has remarked beautifully that-

> "Unparalleled in the history of literature....even when the sun of Hindu religion is set still the love borne for the songs of Vidyapati will never diminish."[4]

Vidyapati was a contemporary of great writers like Chaucer, Shankaradeva, Suradas, Ramanand Roy, Kabir, Chandidas and several others. The historical poetry in vernacularised Avahatta which were written by Vidyapati stands like a link between modern vernacular and Magadhi Prakrit. No other writer can attain his exalted style of lyrical poetry and narrative. He was unique in describing things and representing facts. He is marvelous in describing Jaunpur and nearby areas. His metaphors, similes, alliterations in describing the whores of that area are bold enough to represent realities and attract readers from different horizons. His use of sentences is also unique and well marked. *Kirtilata* is one of the finest creations of the poet. We can say that the age of Vidyapati was the golden period for Mithila and all its nearby territories. He was not simply a man of words but a man of action also. In his real life he was a very helpful person who always stood on the expectations of his friends. He was a staunch realist and he always laid stress on creativity of art. In *Purusha-pariksha* we can see his ideas on diplomacy. To him topics like sex were never a taboo but a reality of life. According to his ideas, there was nothing wrong in writing on such a topic which deals with fundamental urge of a person. His fame and universality lies undoubtedly on *Padavali* which has varying range of songs which is really amazing. The chief characteristic features of its songs lies in its freshness of its style and music. We can find all kinds of songs like riddles, devotional songs, love songs, occasional songs in *Padavali*. We can say that it is a curious mixture of different moods which forms different kind of lyrics and music. He is excellent and unparalleled in describing the youthful beauty, of gestures and movements, of charming poses, of harmonious limbs and divine heart purely filled with love. These creations were an outcome of occasional demands. Without any artificial adornment or external decoration the narrative style is simple but refreshing. There is a kind of contradicting experiences which can be found in longing and remorse, respective and sensuous moods, pathetic and passionate sentiments, enjoyment and propriety and several others. All these sentiments have been depicted in a sophisticated way and with a charming language. He is adept enough in describing beautifully the consummation of love near the river banks or in the lap of nature. He also describes beautifully the pranks of the lover and the beloved. In his ornate style of writing, we can witness nature in the background everywhere. It seems that the mood of the nature matches the human sentiments in almost all of his poetries. We have already seen that his poems of separation are exalted enough to be taken at Himalayan heights. A lover is in anguish and he cannot see that his real conditions and physical appearances are withering. His occasional songs and riddles originate from the real society as if they were the needs of the people. There are different riddles and different songs for different situations of life. It is the harmony of artistic beauty and perfection that his poems appeals the senses and amuses the readers. He has written a beautiful song on rain it says-

> "My friend, there is no limit to my unhappiness
> It is the month of Bhadra, It is raining heavily, and my house is empty.
> The thunder is roaring, and the earth is filled with rain.
> My lover is away in foreign land, and the cruel Kama is darting sharp
> Arrows at me.
> Delighted by the thunder, the peacocks are dancing wildly,
> the frogs are cracking madly, and Dahuki is crying,
> Breaking my heart.
> How will you spend this night without Hari?"[5]

In Eastern India, he was considered as one of the greatest poet who influenced several other writers of the Padas chiefly in respect of diction and style. Looking at his stylistic features, we can say that sometimes he is archaic and sometimes difficult and obscure. The genius of his poetry lies in the fact that he is very close to the subject matter or we can say that he is very subjective in nature. He makes his poetry great only by understanding the true subject matter and depicting it in a beautiful language. The feelings of Radha cannot be felt totally by the readers but it can be understood by the following lines-

> "How shall I tell what I feel?
> My love becomes new every moment
> Ever since my birth have I beheld his beauty
> Yet any eyes are not appeased.
> For millions of ages, have I passed my heart to his
> Yet my heart is not appeased."[6]

The above lines show his greatness because he has embedded a human note which was not exactly known to the vernacular literature. The above lines reflect human love as an offering to another human being in terms of its value as it is abstract. Apart from the allegorical settings these poems are the best examples of love poems. The lyrical tendency has also been heightened and it can be felt if sung individually or in group. He had many titles as if they were like a crown for him. They were Rajapandita, Dasavadhana, Kaviranjana, Kaviratna, Navakavisekhra, Kavisekhra, Abhinavavayadeva, Kanthahara and several others. It is very interesting to find that the eyes of Radha have been compared to different other things like Lotus and bee. The following lines are worth quoting here-

> "the pupil of her eye is like a bee resting on the lotus, the breeze driving it into a corner....the pupil of her eye is like a bee so intoxicated with the honey of the lotus that it cannot fly away."[7]

To the literature of India during the period of fourteenth century these songs written by Vidyapati were new and fresh. They deviated away from the formal poems, and thus, they evoke successfully a very standard poetic convention. Although, he wrote in Maithili but there are a number of images, metaphors and similes which can be seen even in Sanskrit literature. It enchanted not only the people living in villages but also the learned men. Most of the images and symbols used by Vidyapati are fresh and it seems that they have their own individuality. Thus, there are also several techniques implied by Vidyapati which invokes freshness of poetry and creativity has not been compromised. He has used unique images in his poems because these images are taken from numerous sources like contemporary life, nature, court, law, business, literature, mythology and several others. It is interesting to see that no image is too appealing, low or too sublime. There can be some fanciful images but it suits the subject matter or the content of the poem. His songs are very popular even today as they are meant to be sung anywhere as there are varieties of songs. His similes and metaphors are undoubtedly taken from Sanskrit literature but there are several instances where he has gone beyond them. The extraordinary sensibility and the power to express them in form of music males this poet great and we are bound to say that he was far ahead of his time. None of his contemporaries has the power to match his creations and ideas. The use of carnal symbols and images in the devotional poems or songs shows the artistic beauty and boldness of the poet. The image driven by geometry shows the artistic perfection of the poet. Sometimes his lyric seems very dramatic. They are an outcome of specific situations which are filled with a sense of realism. In *padavali* there are several dramatic elements. Vidyapati as a poet of love is unique and nobody can match him in this field. He had given special words to all the female personalities of his poem. We are happy to know that they are not marginalized but they have been understood well by the readers. He himself shows the feminine aspects related to him while expressing the sentiments of a female. It adds natural beauty to his poems and songs.

Vidyapati is famous for several works like *Kirtilata, Kirtipataka, Likhanavali, Vyadhibhaktitarangani, Danavakyavali, Gayapatalaka, Varshakritya, Durgabhaktitarangani, Vibhagasara, Gangavakyavali,*

Saivasarvasvasara, Purushapariksha, Bhuparikrama, including dramas like *Go rakshavijaya and Manimanjari* and several others. He has written several devotional songs. According to some scholars, it is believed that he believed that the motive of all religions is one and that is to attain peace. To him the unity of Godhead matters a lot. He also followed Shakti as a sustainer and nourisher of life and earth. When he describes the charms of Radha in physical form it becomes crystal clear that he is getting his inspirations from the Shakti form of Radha. Thus he was a kind of person who never distinguished between Gods. He believed in one Almighty and wrote accordingly his poems. He is generally acknowledged as a Shaiva by different scholars but it is not logical. After close reading his books, we come across a generalized view that his mental horizons were very broad and his beliefs were very rational. There are several British poets whose thoughts matches with Vidyapati but nobody could match him, it is also a reality. We also know that the age of Vidyapati witnessed the rise of English literature with Chaucer as one of the most prominent writer of this age. We can notice that the second half of the fourteenth Century witnessed several events like the Statute of Servants in 1349, The Black Death of 1348-9, The Peasant Revolt in 1381 and many others. The era covers the whole life span of Chaucer. In The Canterbury Tales we can see the religious view of Chaucer. His scepticism towards religion seems praiseworthy as he approaches towards the real situations of Church during that period of time. G.K Chesterton remarks about Chaucer that-

> "Chaucer's irony was too formless to be noticed. Chaucer is sublimely sly, whether in expressing his own pathos, or in acknowledging his authentic literary precursors, Dante and Boccaccio. Boccaccio particularly made Chaucer possible, in some of the same ways Chaucer enabled Shakespeare to people a world. Chaucer's tales are about tale telling; because Boccaccio had perfected the kind of fiction that is aware of itself as fiction. Stories rhetorically conscious that they are Rhetoric behaves very differently from stories that mask such consciousness. Clearly, Chaucer's heightened sense of story has some relation, however evasive, to the *Decameron*. Chaucer likes to site imaginary authorities, while avoiding any mention of Boccaccio, but that returns us to Chaucerian irony."[8]

Thus, we can see that Chaucer too was very critical from his insight. In several of his works he has written about Church and its function. From the core of his heart he was not happy with the rampant corruption which was common with the clergy men. Either it is Pope himself or the Summoner or the pardoner, almost all the papal authorities were corrupt. P.G.Ruggiers also says that

> "the middle ages manage to salvage the ancient gods by accommodating them into their own customs and beliefs."[9]

We will not be surprised by knowing the fact that in Chaucer's age, Bible was accepted as literal truth and in spite of the rampant corruption in the Church premises, no body dared to challenge it. But, it is also true that although there was Biblical supremacy all around in Chaucer's mind there was a "gnawing doubt"[10]. This doubt hints at the rampant corruption and In the Prologue of *The Legend of Good Women* Chaucer expresses explicitly the doubt and confusion about the literal truth of the holy Church as thought by the theologians. It is worth quoting here-

> "A thousand tymes have I herd men telle
> That ther ys joy in hevene and peyne in helle,
> And I acorde wel that it ys so;
> But, natheless, yet wot I wel also
> That ther nis noon dwellyng in this contree,
> That eyther hath in hevene or helle ybe."[11]

A thousand times it has been mentioned in several folk stories that in hell the sinner can feel pain and in heaven there is only joy and pleasure; it is also correct that on this earth there is hardly any person who can tell us about the experiences of heaven or hell. Chaucer was a kind of person who always believed "for a time in the reality of astral influence, and, in God's use of to bring about his effects in the world."[12]

Now, it becomes crystal clear that Chaucer was a kind of person who never saw things at their face value. He had an insight to judge different things according to his own ways. Comparing his beliefs with the beliefs of Vidyapati we can notice that in Vidyapati there is a kind of scepticism where as in Chaucer we can also feel varying degree of scepticism. Both these poets are great in their own ways and both of them cares for reality. Thus, in both of them, we can find that there is a quest for realism. The motive of Chaucer was not to correct the prevailing system of religion neither we can see it in Vidyapati. These writers believed in presenting things as they are looked upon by them. We have discussed it earlier also that several scholars say that Vidyapati was a follower of Shaivism but if he was a follower of Shaivism he could have never written on the sensual topics covering the aspects of feminism. He was definitely not a hardcore follower of Shaivism but he always considered God as a single form of Shakti. Thus, we can say that these poets were very much self capable in analyzing different forms of religion and life. It can also be seen in the poets like William Langland who is famous for his allegory *Piers Plowman* which has various religious themes. The literary critics who are abided by such ideologies may treat such kind of individuals as a self contained unit. According to Lee Patterson-

> "Understood not as conditioned by social practices and institutions but as an autonomous being who creates the historical world through self-directed efforts."[13]

It does not mean that for poets like William Langland institutions like Churches are secondary to the prior entity of the self. Langland and Chaucer, both write about society whereas in Vidyapati we can see that his poems are social yet very personal not only for himself but for the readers also. I mean to say that when he writes about the love anguish of Radha, we come across the glimpse of the society of Mithila during that time. As a reader, we too get involved in the love anguish of ourselves. His devotional songs are unlike Chaucer and Langland yet there are some similarities. The intensity of irony is less in the writing of Chaucer than Langland as the latter is bitter in tone. In *Miller's tale* of Chaucer, we are surprised to see that there are repeated juxtapositions of sacred and sexual elements in a text. The courting of Alison by Nicholas is a kind of parody where as the parish clerk, Absolon sings love songs in the hope of "midnight tryst"[14]. Critics can charge it as a genuine form of blasphemy or some cheerful Bawdry. Thus there is a kind of dualism in his writings which readers can find easily. In Piers Plowman we can find beautiful themes like "do well and do better"[15]. This poem is the mixture of theological allegory and also a social satire. Here, we can see the religious beliefs of William Langland. Comparing his beliefs with the beliefs of Vidyapati we can once again see that Vidyapati excels in his religious beliefs not because he has not satirized the religion which he talks about but because he is perfect in wring devotional songs. His art of writing differs in style and subject matter, but we cannot refuse that he has written on several serious issues. While writing devotional songs he talks about the ways, one can find peace. His songs are not just poems but they act as a source of inspiration for many young writers of India. He has been translated in other languages also. In the present work, each and every details of his love poems will be analyzed minutely. It will be a fun in comparing Vidyapati with British poets because Vidyapati is a kind of poet who has talked on almost each and every aspect of love, which the modern British poets are still talking.

NOTES AND REFERENCES

1. Muni, Bharta. *Natya Shastra*, Facsimile Publisher, Delhi, 2013, p.1-2

2. https://en.wikipedia.org/wiki/Platonic_love

3. Sidney, Philip. *Astrophiland Stella*, Kessinger Publishing, Montana, 2010. p.5

4. Choudhary, Radha Krishna. *A Survey of Maithili Literature*, Shruti Publications, Delhi, 1976, p.58
5. ibid, p.59
6. ibid, p.60
7. ibid.
8. (Bloom's critical views: Geoffrey Chaucer, 2007: 11)
9. Gardner, J. *The Life and Times of Geoffrey Chaucer*, Vintage Books, New York, 1977.p. 7
10. Whittock, T. *A Reading of The Canterbury Tales*, Cambridge University Press, Cambridge, 1968.p.115
11. https://books.google.co.in/books?isbn=0199552096
12. Gardner, J. *The Life and Times of Geoffrey Chaucer*, Vintage Books, New York, 1977.p.18
13. Patterson, Lee '*Historical Criticism and the Development of Chaucer Studies*', University of Wisconsin Press, 1987, Madison. p.19
14. As observed by Helen Cooper 'motifs of the Flood and the 'legende' of a carpenter and his wife are secularized to a point of blasphemy. The Canterbury Tales, Oxford Guides to Chaucer (Oxford, 1989), p.101.
15. https://en.wikipedia.org/wiki/Piers_Plowman

****

Chapter Two

The love tradition an observation

Although, the word Love looks very simple but it is not an easy task to write on this subject. It encompasses different mental and emotional states ranging from pleasure to varying interpersonal affections. The very first understanding of love can be personal attraction or strong attachment. Different scholars have also agreed that it can also be a kind of virtue which is the embodiment of human kindness, affection or compassion. Greek philosophers have classified Love in different forms like divine love, romantic love, friendly love and familial love. As the age advanced the concept of Love also broadened like courtly love, self love, infatuated love came into prominence. Apart from such concepts, spiritual or religious love was kept in different category. To make and strengthen inter personal relationships, Love is very necessary and it has a psychological importance too which will be dealt further. To keep the human beings united and continue different forms of life, Love plays a very key and functional role. The essence or nature of Love is a matter of debate as it is very tough for the scholars to agree on a single point of view. Different people have different concepts on a single topic. The generalized view of love can be felt as an outlet of positive sentiment but a stronger form of dislike or hate also gives the idea of a neutral apathy. It is very interesting to see that the physical intimacy or bodily attachment related to Love is also connected to lust. It is also correct that love and lust are quiet opposite to each other yet they are connected. The love as an abstract form is nothing but individual experience which a person feels for the other. It can also be love for the self or narcissism. With the passage of time, understanding of Love and idea associated with it has also changed drastically. The ancient love poetries flourished even in the middle ages and after it Courtly love rose into prominence. The impersonal theory of love says that there can be love for some objects, animals, goal or principle which can be of great value. The bonding or love between human beings can be referred as interpersonal love. This kind of love is unique form of relationship and it can be seen between members of a family, couples or friends. Psychologically Love can be referred as a social characteristic. Robert Sternberg, a very famous psychologist has formulated a special theory of Love which is triangular in nature. He has argued that there are three components of Love- Passion, commitment and intimacy. He has defined intimacy as a segment of love in which two individuals share every minute detail of their lives. It can be seen in romantic love affairs or some close friendship. In such kind of relationships commitment acts like a driver which can drive the relationship permanently. Now coming back to the love tradition, we will find that Petrarch was a mile stone for special kind of love and in his sonnets we can also find that Neo platonic love has been redefined. The primary source from which we can start the love convention is *Rerum vulgarium fragmenta* which is the collection of poems. In 1327, Petrarch began to write and collect poems of his interest. In the whole series, we can find that there are love poems which are addressed to a beautiful lady whose name was Laura. She was so beautiful that the poet was infatuated with her, it will not be wrong saying that the lady was actually a kind of inspiration for the poet. Several scholars doubt whether she was real or just an imagination of the poet because she has been described beautifully. The poems end in the form of a hymn to the Blessed virgin as we are informed that Laura dies. In the words of Robert W. Durling-

> "Petrarch's lover completes three times a cycle that takes him through falling in love, hoping and wooing, being rejected and rebuked and finally lamenting and writing poetry."[1]

We are reminded by Durling that there were traditional themes in the writings of Petrarch. In the love conventions mentioned by Durling it is clear that the chief concern of this poet was the ideally beautiful lady who is not only beautiful but virtuous too. It is very interesting to see that the frustration, love sickness of the lover and obsessive yearning parallels to the feudal system where there is a master and a slave. The kind of relationship between the lover and the beloved is not exactly like the relationship between a master and a slave but it is also not less then that. The lover thinks that it is his duty to admire and follow his beloved. He takes delight while doing so because it amuses both his mind as well as his soul. For Petrarch his beloved Laura is the paragon of perfection, such kind of qualities can also be seen later in the sonnets of Shakespeare. Although, the style of writing is different in Shakespeare but still he has tried to write on such beautiful subject matter. Here, it seems that the perfection of Laura is inseparable with her beauty. Kenelm Foster says that-

> "The idea of a supreme source of beauty which though transcendent fills all things with its omnipresence, which cannot be escaped by any flight, mirrors...the relation of God to the universe and to the human soul, as described in the speak of Dante in the opening lines of the Paradiso."[2]

We have already stated that apart from being beautiful, Laura is also virtuous and so she is the reflection of divinity for Petrarch. This divinity is a notion which is connected with the Neo Platonic love. Peter Hainsworth has beautifully studied that there was something parallel between Renaissance Neo Platonists and Petrarch. Both of them associates beauty and virtue with the image of light

> "In general terms Laura's beauty takes on positive associations through being evoked in images which suggest light or brightness. Characteristically she enlightens, clarifies, illumines. She is a star, though the second of the two sestine ... is exceptional in that it associates her with the moon. Much more frequently she is like the sun, or is the sun, or is brighter than the sun"[3]

Laura's eyes have also been compared to stars and later the comparison becomes more allusive in nature. It is noteworthy

to find that Vidyapati has also compared the beauty of Radha with farfetched imagery. Thus, there is a sense of similarity between these two poets. Shakespeare has also written on the same subject matter but his sense of comparison is a little bit different. According to Vidyapati Krishna is elder than Radha . The beauty of Radha also signifies that she is no more a child and thus she has become an epitome of beauty. Her smile is sweet and her lips are also described as coral lips. Her steps are very gentle and whenever she touches the ground with her feet water lilies spring up. No doubt it is an exaggeration but the beauty of the poem lies in the heightened form of poetic imagination. It is also very interesting to see that she is conscious about her womanly charm and thus she is unable to hide it as nobody can suppress beauty. This dawn of blissful youth has been described well in *Vayasandhi*. Coming back to Petrarch, we have already seen that he expresses his gratitude towards Laura by praising her eyes which are the guiding stars for him. Aldo S. Bernado has beautifully remarked that-

> "The irreproachable conduct of Laura inspired him to superimpose a Christian view of the woman on his beloved. He thus began to endow his image of Laura with the characteristics necessary to convert her into a lady-guide to the Christian heaven."[4]

To the celestial realm, she becomes a guide after her death but she was a source of inspiration for the poet all the time. Even after her death Petrarch has made her immortal, describing her virtues and beauty. There is a kind of interrelationship between the beloved's virtues, beauty and the lover's state of approach to seek her every minute glaze has been stated by Nicholas Kilmer who says that-

> "Petrarch had adopted the Courtly Love tradition literally and sincerely. That tradition required his amorous attachment to a woman who, because she was already married and was irrevocably chaste, was unattainable; but who at the same time, since she was above all virtuous and beautiful, should lead the poet to the contemplation of still higher beauty--the Perfect Beauty. This, being divine, was incorporeal; and being incorporeal was both absolutely beautiful and invisible. Perfect Beauty was none other than God Himself, and the virtuous life His love and care demanded."[5]

This is also true that the beloved is not attainable, is the central theme in many of the love poems written by different poets in different ages. Laura was already married and thus she was not attainable for the poet. In Padavali, the poet, Vidyapati has written various songs of different moods, we have already discussed it yet his sensuousness related to feminine beauty is marvelous. He has tried to define almost every aspect of beauty. In the western world, Platonism is the most influential traditions of love. It flourished through the great writers like Aristotle and Plotinus. During the age of neo Platonism, it was revived. In the middle ages, the courtly love and the nineteenth century witnessed Romanticism. These forms of love are deep rooted in Platonic love. In modern times, it is interpreted as non physical relationship between heterosexual individuals. Aristophanes, the great playwright had explained this form of love through comical and colourful truth that love is nothing but it is a kind of quest for the alter ego. It is a kind of remedy against the wound which has been given to the mankind by God. Socrates too affirms the theory of Aristophanes but adds a little that love is our search for goodness. According to him, the only object of love is goodness. Here Plato has given the definition of love he says that it is a kind of desire which always looks ahead for possessing good. In his own words "Love is desire for the perpetual possession of the good."[6] It becomes clear from this definition that love is first of all a kind of desire but this desire is for the objects which are good in life. Thus, goodness has been objectified but goodness is never an object. For every individual the definition of goodness is not same. Plato also believes in the fact that it is not only the human beings who are in search of goodness but the entire universe is approaching towards doing good and searching good. Thus, the whole world or universe is in love and it can also be one reason that the whole world is round or united to each other. Without love, existence of anything can be doubted. Thus, all things are in love and we human beings are conscious enough to search beauty and goodness. According to this theory, everybody is ignorant and they are incapable to love as goodness keeps on changing towards perfection. Nothing is permanent so our quest for goodness is also not fixed. The hunt for goodness is always on. If it is right then why do men and women marry? Can marriage guarantee the permanent goodness of our partner? Thus this love is a question that if the quest for goodness is love then love is certainly not attainable. The matter becomes more complex when we say that goodness which has been attained can never be love itself as the quest for goodness is changing continuously in search of perfection. This perfection is a kind of object like goodness which can never be attained. We cannot leave the topic in between as the goodness lies in searching the answer of this question which is a kind of analysis of Platonic love. Scholars have argued that the goodness is the desire to live forever to cherish the life. Thus, there is a desire for immortality. This is one of the reasons that love is the key cause for reproduction of the species, that is, to say that any individual may cease to be alive but his offspring's continue to live. Thus, life never ends but it becomes immortal. In the *Republic* the author Plato has mentioned that –

> "He contemplates a world of unchanging and harmonious order, where reason governs and nothing can do or suffer wrong; and like one who imitates an admired companion, he cannot fail to fashion himself in its likeness. So the philosopher, in constant companionship with the divine order of the world, will reproduce that order in his soul and, so far as man can, become godlike; though here, as elsewhere, there will be scope for detraction."[7]

According to Plato human nature is of dualistic view that is to say that body can be mortal but the soul is always immortal. Before possessing a body soul lived with God but when a physical body is granted to a soul then the soul forgets its divinity. It is not so simple to understand but we may think that there must be a path of love. Love is never blind; a lover first of all contemplates the physical presence of the beloved. There are several problems and difficulties. There are contradictions in his point of views towards homosexuality. His views are also not genuine, at some point when we study his attitude towards women. I am not going to discuss all those points in detail as the present topic covers only the love traditions an observation, but this kind of tradition was certainly not applicable everywhere that is why there are various modifications in his theory. Our understanding of Plato is not finished as there are several other issues also but as the age advanced Petrarchan culture of love once again rose into prominence. Applying all the known love traditions to Petrarch he says continuously that Laura is the brightest star. He keeps on praising his beloved as if he is going to attain some spirituality by praising his lady love. In this context, Bernado has beautifully mentioned that-

> "Laura emerge[s] as that inspiration that is at the heart of all true poetry. She is, in short, the inspiration that moves poets and men of letters to literary expression, an image of beauty and truth. It was for this reason that Petrarch was able to retain Laura as a beautiful, vibrant woman whose spirit remained with him on this earth even after death. She is as a Christian Daphne to a Christian Apollo."[8]

Now coming to another tradition of love we can see that there flourished courtly love tradition which has influenced several poets to write on the love affairs and love themes. In 1883, Gaston Paris has coined this term Courtly love in one of the very famous journal of the age entitled *Romania*. In middle ages, this kind of concept was very new so it attracted the poets as well as the readers. Some scholars believed that it evolved from Southern France. It has a new structure which was very different from feudalism and the Christian beliefs. In terms of diction or the use of words there are some similarities between the Church languages and courtly form of love. It is not like the chivalric romance or the kind of love which we can notice in knighthood heroism but rather it was very sophisticated and refined. There is hardly any form of violence or bloodshed. There is respect and admiration for the beloved which the lover shows. It is courtly because it followed the courtly culture. The close reading of courtly love tradition certainly gives us an idea that it was an extension of Petrarchan love tradition. It heightens the status of the beloved or the women. It is a kind of code of conduct which was very popular in the aristocracies of Western Europe. It was a kind of vassal-lord relationship where a knight was considered as an obedient servant of his beloved. There is no violence yet the knight could go to any extent to win the favour of his lady love. It was often secret and outside wedlock. Here also, it was almost impossible for the lover to attain or possess his beloved. Some scholars argue that it was a kind of dignified form of adultery. It was well defined in the French and English royal courts presided generally by the crown. Throughout Europe, it was very popular which influenced several young writers to write on this convention. Before approaching to the next love convention, we should give a close analysis of the origination of Sonnet. Several historians have pointed out that Sir Thomas Wyatt has borrowed this form of writing from Italians. During that period of time, this form of writing was a kind of vehicle for expressing the personal feelings and emotions. It conveyed the message of a lover to his beloved which can be personal in tone. It is interesting to see that it was the most popular form of writing during the early sixteenth century. Wyatt himself has not written any kind of Sonnets which is popular or memorable, but he has started the tradition of writing Sonnets. He has started imitating Petrarch and thus he initiated bold images and new ideas to be written into English. The name of Surrey is as important to be mentioned as Thomas Wyatt. Both of them are jointly remembered to popularize this form of writing into English. Moving forward, we can notice that English sonneteers introduced several changes while writing Sonnets. The Sonnet length was not altered, but its content and form was changed. We are already aware of *Astrophel and Stella* written by Sir Philip Sidney. It was largely autobiographical in nature and the subject matter is again a kind of love, where the lover finds his lady love not attainable. Sidney was himself in love with a girl of nineteen who was married to another man and thus his love was unattainable. These sonnets are magical as it covers the sensual and passionate desire of the lover. Spenser has written a Sonnet sequence entitled *Amoretti*. In this sequence, we can find eighty eight Sonnets and it was published in 1595. I am writing about Sonnets because they were very popular and it became a traditional form of writing which is specially remembered for conventional love. They were no doubt conventional, yet fresh, because it appealed to the readers. The Sonnets written by Spenser are also autobiographical in tone. Spenser was in love with a woman whose name was Elizabeth Boyle whom he got married. These Sonnets are very frank and melancholic and we feel a sensitive delight while reading such poems. Later, we can find that Shakespeare has also written 154 Sonnets and these Sonnets are written with a different form, these sonnets are addressed to a friend and a dark lady. Elizabethan Sonnets are incomplete without mentioning the name of Shakespeare. The close reading of Shakespearean sonnets gives us another idea of love tradition which is praiseworthy. There is a kind of lyricism in the sonnets of Shakespeare which is unlike other sonneteers. If we look closely, his sonnet number two, we can find it lyrical as well as emotional. Here, the poet has praised the beauty of his friend and he also wants that this kind of beauty should be perpetuated even in the offspring of his friend if ever he gets married. This kind of thinking is not common and it hints the kind of love tradition during the time of Shakespeare. None of his contemporary has written on such subject matter. His intentions are very clear in his sonnets, we can find three quatrains and a couplet which is again a new kind of writing. He has used rhyme in the quatrains as well as in the couplet which is a kind of contribution to its lyricism. The rhythm of the poem also provides a perfect blending of the lyricism and the subject matter. The use of phrases, words and the language itself suggests the readers that the concept of love was very liberal, during the Elizabethan period. In sonnet number three, the poet again admires the beauty of his friend. He argues that no woman can resist the beauty of his friend. He says that his friend reflects his mother's beauty. It is the heightened form of emotion which can be seen in the form of male bonding. It is also noteworthy that during the time of Petrarch the beauty was considered as an object of the beloved. He has praised the beauty of the woman and even in the poems of Vidyapati, we can see that he too admires the beauty of Radha but he also writes about the features of Krishna that he was a lord who was very handsome. Here in Shakespeare, we can see the form of male bonding which is not common. Thus with the flow of time the form of writing in terms of subject matter has also changed. The following lines convey the ideas of the poet beautifully-

"Look in thy glass and tell the face thou viewest,
Now is the time that face should form another,
Whose fresh repair if now thou not renewest,
Thou dost beguile the world, un bless some mother.
For where is she so fair whose uneared womb."[9]

Such lines tell us about the friend of Shakespeare whom he admired the most. It is also a kind of love which can be understood as a form of male bonding. Few scholars have also said that it is a kind of homosexuality, and that is why, Shakespeare has written about his friend. He has a homosexual relationship with his friend. In the words of Robert Giroux-

> "The evidence against overtness is the stronger evldence due to the repeated identification of beauty and virtue. Infidelity in these poems is to turn from virtue to stain. To have written Sonnet 144, 'Two loves I have, of comfort and despair,' with its religious notes opposing the holy love for his friend to the profane love of the dark lady, in order to mask an overt homosexual relationship, is a little hard to imagine. One could argue against this that one may be idealistic about a physical affair or point to Shakespeare's capacity for rationalization. Again, perhaps so, but again not probably so. While Elizabethans could be sophisticated about overt homosexuality, as in the coy passages in Marlowe's Hero and Leander . . . it is a long way from that to making overt homosexuality a standard of purity."[10]

So far, we have seen that in the love poems the lover feels that following his beloved is his ultimate task as he admires his beloved. This kind of love can be seen in the courtly love tradition. In Petrarchan love tradition, we have seen that the lover finds his beloved as his guiding star and thus it is the duty of the lover to follow his beloved. By doing this the lover makes an ascent. He realizes the beauty of his own soul and it is also correct that the lover is incomplete without his beloved. He imagines his beloved all around him and thus in this way he tries to complete himself. By doing so, the lover tries to attain a kind of sublimity which is pure. In the words of Castiglioni-

> "among all these blessings the lover will find one that is far greater still, if he will determine to make use of this love as a step by which to climb to another that is far more sublime; and this will be possible if he continually reflects how narrowly he is confined by always limiting himself to the contemplation of a single body. And so in order to escape from this confinement, he will gradually add so many adornments to his idea of beauty that, by uniting all possible forms of beauty in his mind, he will form a universal concept and so reduce all the many varieties to the unity of that single beauty which sheds itself over human nature as a whole."[11]

In the time of Milton, we can see that the concept of love was again redefined. In *Paradise Lost*, Milton says that Eve was beautiful and Adam loved him a lot but she was inferior to her husband, Adam. She was beautiful yet inferior but we cannot deny that she was also a kind of guiding star for Adam. Several critics have said that it was she, not Adam who was responsible for the damnation as she prompted Adam to commit the universal sin. If she was not inferior then why Satan has selected only her, not Adam to execute his planning. He was aware that Adam was the favourite of God so it was almost impossible to persuade him to eat the fruit of the forbidden tree. The act of love making has been seen by Milton as sacred and that is why Satan was envious and full of rage. In almost every religion including Christianity, love is considered as the most important attribute of the almighty which is gifted to the human kind. After the creation of Adam it was considered by God that Adam can think like him. God has created him on the last day only to admire the world and the beauty of God which he has shown in creating the nature. Adam is intelligent and full of wisdom and it was one of the reasons that he wanted Eve to be created so that Eve can also admire and love him. Love is in center and Eve was created from his own body part so we can say that Adam's love for Eve was love for his own self. Milton was a radical writer and he has suggested that Adam and Eve had physical relations before punishment as it was sinless in his eye. He shows us a kind of marital love which is pure and innocent. It also involves sexuality but it is a kind of obedience to the almighty who has commanded it to be fruitful. It is very interesting to see that Milton has also suggested a kind of hierarchy in marriage. Husband is more superior to the wife and that is why Adam can communicate with God directly, whereas Eve is considered as weak as she can communicate with God only through her husband, Adam. Although, *Paradise Lost* is a poem which is considered as a religious poem but there are several love expressions in this poem. Adam knows that Eve is weak and that is why he never leaves her alone, but Eve cannot understand it and she persuades him to allow her to work alone. This loneliness of Eve is utilized by the Satan and he successfully convinces her to eat the fruit of the forbidden tree. Adam knows that it is dangerous to eat the forbidden fruit of knowledge, God's wrath will fall upon them yet he does it because he really loved Eve. This sacrifice for Eve is the sacrifice for love and the loss cannot be compensated. We have already discussed that Eve was created by the body parts of Adam so if Adam loves Eve, then it is his narcissistic desire. Now a question arises that is there anything common between the writings of Vidyapati and Milton. Both of them are great poets of their own time, yet there are some similarities between them. Vidyapati has also written several devotional poems and there are instances of love even in his religious poems. Religion and love cannot be separated as both of them are two different wheels of the same vehicle. In Adam, we can see that he cannot tolerate separation as it gives a feeling of rejection. Separation is said to increase the intensity of love which has been also written by Vidyapati in the poems of Virah Vedna. It is noteworthy to find that the rejection of God is possible for Adam but he cannot leave her beloved, Eve alone. It is a unique feature of love which rationalizes the guilt of the lover and the beloved but love itself is never guilty. To love the commands of God is the duty of Adam but to leave heaven for the sake of his beloved, Eve is also the command of God. It seems that the beauty of the Paradise is not enough to match the beauty of Eve and that can be one of the reasons that even in hell, Adam cannot leave the hands of Eve. There is much dissimilarity between the writings of John Milton and Vidyapati, yet there are similarities between the tone and intensity of expression. Quoting few lines from Book IX can put some more light on the topic as Adam understands that even in death they will be unified and it will be an honoured death in comparison to a lonely life-

> "However I with thee have fixed my lot,
> Certain to undergo like doom; if death
> Consort with thee, death is to me as life;
> So forcible within my heart I feel
> The bond of nature draw me to my own,
> My own in thee, for what thou art is mine;
> Our state cannot be severed, we are one,
> One flesh; to lose thee were to lose myself."[12]

These lines clearly express that Milton understands the value of emotions and he also tries to express the religious views of a lover who likes to be damned together with his beloved than to live single in the Garden of Paradise. The love poetries of John Donne can prove it more clearly as he is a kind of writer who glorifies love. He is often known as a metaphysical poet who often uses farfetched imagery in his poems. The scope and variety of love poems written by John Donne is remarkable. In his writings, we can find a sense of dualism between holy love and physical love. His greatness lies in the fact that he beautifully makes a balance between these two forms of love. He also has faith upon the sanctity of marriage. It is noteworthy to see that during his time writing love poems was a kind of fashion or we can say that it was a kind of fashionable exercise. He was perfect in writing love poems and it is interesting to see that his poems are very different from the Elizabethan love poems. His depth of feeling and use of fascination is unique. In his poems, we can see that less stress has been given to beauty and aesthetic elements are also less in terms of passion. His poems are sensual in nature which attracts readers and they are delighted in reading such sensuousness. Sentiment and tenderness are also less; in his poems there is a kind of infiniteness in lover's heart who pleads to the beloved that she should love him from the bottom of her heart. He pleads that not a part of her heart is required but he needs complete heart to love him. He does not believe in loving in parts. He demands complete concentration and this is the beauty of the poet that his sensuality is unique. We cannot find such a kind of sensuality in other poets. This art of writing is rarely found. There are almost three strands in his poetry. First one is cynical, which is sometime hostile to women. The theme turns towards the frailty of man which was a kind of advantage for lovers who were in search of extra marital relationships. He also talks often about married life which is happy when it is loyal and true. In poems like *A Valediction*, we can find such themes. There is also some kind of Platonic strand in his poems. In *The Canonization*, we can see this form of love. Here love has been treated as a holy emotion which is to be worshipped both by the lover as well as the beloved. His treatment of love is not idealistic but realistic. He is very practical in approach as well as understanding of love. He establishes a kind of relationship between the soul and the body which is pure and real. True love is not just bodily love, but it is a kind of relationship between body as well as the soul to the other soul. In *A Valediction: a forbidding mourning*, we can find that only physical union is not necessary. He hardly describes the physical beauty of the beloved however it is very surprising that a poet who talks often about physical union is not describing the female beauty. We have seen both Shakespeare and John Donne writing love poems but both of them are far apart from each other in terms of era as well as content. No doubt both of them are fine poets and both of them write about love but their concepts varies sometimes. We can notice such variations several times but there are some similarities too. Lines from sonnet number one hundred and thirty written by Shakespeare needs to be quoted here-

> "My mistress' eyes are nothing like the sun;
> Coral is far more red than her lips' red;
> If snow be white, why then her breasts are dun;
> If hairs be wires, black wires grow on her head.
> I have seen roses damask'd, red and white,
> But no such roses see I in her cheeks;
> And in some perfumes is there more delight
> Than in the breath that from my mistress reeks.
> I love to hear her speak, yet well I know
> That music hath a far more pleasing sound;
> I grant I never saw a goddess go;
> My mistress, when she walks, treads on the ground:
> And yet, by heaven, I think my love as rare
> As any she belied with false compare."[13]

These lines clearly reflect the ideology of Shakespeare that his love is rare although the eyes of his mistress do not shine like the sun. Her lips are not red still he loves her. John Donne too believes that describing physical beauty of the beloved is not necessary. Thus, the tradition of courtly love where the beloved was seen like a master and the lover as his slave is no more working here. We cannot say that the intensity of love has defoliated but it has been greatly understood with the passage of time. Love cannot happen at the first sight however there are several view points on this topic. Love must be understood by the lover as well as the beloved. To understand love there is a need of an active mind to judge the intensity of love but unfortunately reason and passion are far apart from each other. A passionate heart hardly cares for any reason. Quoting lines from *The Sun Rising* written by John Donne-

> " Busy old fool, unruly sun,
> Why dost thou thus,
> Through windows, and through curtains call on us?
> Must to thy motions lovers' seasons run?
> Saucy pedantic wretch, go chide
> Late school boys and sour prentices,
> Go tell court huntsmen that the king will ride,
> Call country ants to harvest offices,
> Love, all alike, no season knows nor clime,
> Nor hours, days, months, which are the rags of time."[14]

Here, the role of sun is to disturb the lovers and we can see the beauty of John Donne that how successfully he has projected the lover as well as the beloved. Here reason and passion can be seen and felt clearly. Lovers hardly care for any reason. John Donne further writes-

> "Thy beams, so reverend and strong
> Why shouldst thou think?
> I could eclipse and cloud them with a wink,
> But that I would not lose her sight so long;
> If her eyes have not blinded thine,
> Look, and tomorrow late, tell me,"[15]

There is a sudden shift of tone in the poems of Donne and readers can notice it easily. The bright light of the sun can be eclipsed by the wink of eyes and this wink can be felt easily while making love to each other. The other reference to the eyes is also very remarkable as the eyes of the beloved are so powerful that it can make the personified sun blind. It is not sure that Donne might have written that the eyes of the beloved are beautiful, but it cannot be denied that the eyes are powerful. Now coming to the poems written by W.B.Yeats, we can find there are several autobiographical references in his poems. He was in love with a girl whose name was Maud Gonne. She was an actress and daughter of a British Colonel. She was very beautiful and Yeats was very passionate for her. In the twentieth century, Yeats was considered as one of the greatest poets and even today he is often quoted. His concept of love is rare as he is a kind of poet who believes in immortality of love. In his poems, we can see that the inner world and the outer world are coherent to each other. His idea of love tradition is a kind of blend of idealism and realism. Thus, there is a kind of practicality in sense of approach as well as writing. Yeats has written about Maud Gonne that-

> "I thought of your beauty, and this arrow; Made out of a wild thought, is in my marrow; There's no man may look upon her, no man; As when newly grown to be a woman, Tall and noble; but with face and bosom Delicate in colour as apple blossom; This beauty's kinder, yet for a reason; I could weep that the old is out of season."[16]

Yeat's love for Maud Gonne cannot be measured although it was love at the first sight. He has described his first meeting with her lady love like this and it can be traced in one of his love poems *The Arrow*. Maud Gonne has not reciprocated the same love to him and in a response, he has written several love poems dedicated to his love. In July, 1891 Yeats received a letter from Maud Gonne and he considered this letter as a token of love but he was taken aback when she refused his love and said-

> "Poets should never marry. The world should thank me for not marrying you"[17]

From then, she has rejected her thrice and Yeats found himself in a pitiable condition. Finally, she married an Irish army man, McBride. This marriage was a mismatch, and lastly the marriage failed. At this condition also, Yeats proposed her but again she refused. This kind of love is rarely seen as Yeats loved her for his entire life. Thus, we have seen love traditions from different ages and there is something new about love traditions in almost all the ages although the intensity and the passion remains the same. It is also a fact that in this world, there is no any machine to measure love. It is not possible to measure the magnitude of love although we can understand it and feel it. Understanding love is also not an easy task as different rulers and saints have made or ruined their life in love. Poets can give their words to their poetry but sentiments cannot be drawn on paper, however, by reading beautiful love poems we can be moved or transported to an exalted level. Either it is the poems of Shakespeare or the feelings of Plato but this is also a fact that realism of literature needs an assumption. Facts and dates cannot make us understand the concept of love but it is also true that by reading autobiographies through prose or poetry we can understand that love is divine and we cannot attain perfection in love as it is immortal.

NOTES AND REFERENCES

1. Durling Robert M, *Petrarch's Lyric Poems*, Cambridge university press, Harvard, 1976.p.28

2. Foster, Kenelm, *Petrarch Poet and Humanist* (University of Edinburgh press, Edinburgh, 1984.p. 25

3. Hainsworth, Peter, *Petrarch The Poet*, Routledge publishers, New York, 1988. p.122

4. Aldo S. Bernardo, *Petrarch, Laura and the Triumphs* (Albany: State U of New York P, 1974).p. 8.

5. Nicholas, Kilmer, *Songs and Sonnets from Laura's Lifetime* (San Francisco: North Point P, 1981) .p.11

6. https://condor.depaul.edu/dsimpson/tlove/symposium.html

7. (Plato, 1941, p. 208)

8. Aldo, s, Petrarch, *Scipio and the "Africa"* (Baltimore: The Johns Hopkins P, 1962) .p.68

9. http://www.shakespeare-online.com/sonnets/3detail.html

10. Robert Giroux, *The Book Known As Q* (Saddle Brook, New Jersey: McClelland and Stewart Ltd., 1982).p. 31

11. Baldesar Castiglioni, *The Book of The Courtier* (New York: Penguin Books, 1978) .p.338.

12. http://knarf.english.upenn.edu/Milton/pl9.html

13. http://www.shakespeare-online.com/sonnets/130.html

14. https://www.poetryfoundation.org/poems/44129/the-sun-rising
15. ibid.
16. Finneran, Richard J. (1996). *The Collected Works of W.B. Yeats* Volume I: The Poems: Revised Second Edition. Ed. New York: Scribner. p.77
17. Kelly, John and Donville, Eric. (1986).*The Collected Letters of W. B. Yeats*, Vol. I, eds., Oxford: Clarendon Press.p. 54

****

Chapter Three

Style and Features

It is said that literary achievements of Vidyapati has not been touched or reached by any other poets of his age. He has been a source of inspiration for many young writers and scholars. At a time when Maithili Literature was rising at its prominence, then it was thought that in the field of literature it would serve the world as a milestone. Shiva, Shakti and Vishnu were the three popular deities of Mithila and it is interesting to note that Mithila was considered as one of the important centers of spirituality. Vidyapati composed *Shaivasarvasvasara* and *Nachari* and other poems in the honour of Lord Shiva. His style and features are unique and it cannot be found in the any other genres of literature. The devotional songs of Vidyapati have been widely circulated and still today it is often quoted. The most common form of poetry in Mithila is Tirhuti and it has a kind of lyrical expression which is indigenous in nature and origin. It has all the kinds of love affairs in it starting from union to separation of the lover and the beloved. I have not talked about the ending because it is very subjective. If we take separation of the lover and the beloved as its beginning then we cannot say that the unification is the last phase because love gets deeper and deeper in separation. Vidyapati has written several songs and poems on such issues. One of the very famous forms of such kind of writings is Batagamni. It is sung with a melodious voice when heroine or nayika goes to meet her lover. Vidyapati is the most celebrated writer for such kind of poems and songs. Some famous style of writings of such songs are represented by Lagni, Malara, yoga, samadauni and sohara. Samadauni is sung on the occasion of Navaratri and thus it is a kind of adieu to Goddess Durga. One can also bid farewell to his daughter at the time of her marriage by singing such kind of songs. Vidyapati is a kind of writer who is very conscious in choosing words for his poems. He tries to write accurate and matching words for a particular emotion. It is one of the reasons that in his songs there are preferences for tadbhava words. It does not mean that the tatsama words are absent from his songs. Tadbhava words are preferred in his writings because they bring out the linguistic peculiarity of any geographical region and thus it looks more real. During the time of Vidyapati from Gujarat to Bengal Apabhramsa Avahatta was the most famous literary language which had some local variations. There also the tadbhava words are widely used. It is interesting to see that it parallels to the sonnet tradition. The sonnet came out from two strains of language and literature. One is native which started from the feudal courts of province whereas the other started from the regions of thirteenth century Italy. Any provincial reader can find out the images and attitudes which got vanished with the time. The local languages and dialects were changed by the poets and authors according to their own interest. Even Chaucer has tried and experimented linguistic variations in his own writings. In English Literature we can find so many words of different origins. Some are French, some are Italian and it shows that how language evolved in any particular area. With the adaptation of new words the religious views of the people also changed drastically. Language is a kind of identity and if we do some addition or subtraction of words from a particular dialect or language then it also changes the identity of a particular region. Thus there is a constant influence of language over any form of writings. There are occasional touches of gaiety which is a result of surviving lyrics in any genre of literature. It seems that love in the form of poetry has become frail which is pitiable and it is flourishing over the mercy of readers-

"Mirie it is while summer ilast
With fugheles song;
Oc nu necheth windes blast
And weder strong.
Ei, ei, what this nicht is long!
And ich with wel michel wrong
Soreghe and murne and fast."[1]

The above lines are provincial in origin and the poet is feeling sad because it is spring time and he is feeling secluded. The nightingale sings in the moonlight. It seems that the language used is of Troubadours who were famous at the time of Angevin England. With the advancement of time the lyrics also changed. Either it is Maithili Literature or English Literature we can find evolution and there are drastic changes in the use of words, metaphors and similes. I am writing this chapter to encompass style and features used by Vidyapati and some British Poets. In British poets I shall try to compare and contrast poets from different ages. I have already mentioned that Vidyapati followed a very different style of writing but still there are some similarities between him and few British Poets. When I write about the features I mean stylistic features of different poets which I intend to focus in this chapter. While reading the poems of Vidyapati I was surprised to find that there are similarities in terms of style and features between Vidyapati and Romantic poets especially of John Keats. In Endymion John Keats has said that happiness is a state of our mind. It means that our mind has the capacity to decide our happiness and our minds are raised to a certain kind of fellowship filled with essence and we are left alchemized-

> "feel we these things? that moment we have stept
> Into a sort of oneness, and our state
> Is like a fleeting spirit's. But there are
> Richer entanglements, enthrallments far
> More self – destroying, leading by degress
> To the chief intensity."[2]

It is well known to the world that John Keats got carried away into the realms of ecstasy whenever he witnessed the beauty associated with visible things. he was a kind of poet who considered truth as beauty and beauty as truth. In case of Vidyapati we can find that he was also a kind of poet who always gave priority to truth. He was also considered as a sensual poet who wrote several songs and poems on the topics like love and beauty. He has presented a beautiful picture of a beloved in terms of her physicality. She was beautiful enough to make her lover stand alive from his grave.

He has also written devotional songs of Radha and Krishna but to him truth and beauty was always a major concern. The understanding of reality for John Keats was unique. In comparison to William Blake this understanding was narrow. According to Blake the realm of imagination can also be real. Thus William Blake presented an active understanding of reality whereas John Keats presented a passive form of reality. We have already talked about the role of imagination in case of Vidyapati. Truth and beauty are two different things. There can be a truth which can be bitter. This bitter truth is beautiful or not it depends upon the given situation. Sri Aurobindo has translated the poems of Vidyapati into English and in one of the songs he has associated the beauty of a lady with brightness. Few lines from the song needs to be quoted here-

> "How shall I tell of caanou's beauty bright?
> Men will believe it a vision of the night.
> As lightning was his saffron garment blown
> Over the beautiful cloud-limbs half shown
> His coal –black curls assumed with regal grace
> A peacock's plume above that moonlike face.
> And such a fragrance fierce the mad winds wafts
> Love wakes and trembles for his flowery shafts."[3]

The above lines project the clear picture of beauty associated with natural things. It is like a vision of the night. This vision is so clear that it has been associated with the brightness of the nature. Sometimes scholars have also said about Vidyapati that he is a kind of poet who loves to write about nature. This nature is both the nature of the human being as well as the external form of nature. There is a kind of fine balance between the internal as well as the external form of nature. This kind of imagination where the internal form of nature fuses with the external nature is not wild. They are controlled through poetic justice. It is very interesting to see that Coleridge has also justified this by his paradox in one of his letters he has written that-

> "Dare I add that genius must act of the feeling that body is but a striving to become mind- that is mind in its essence."[4]

It is to be noted here that there are not much comparisons between Coleridge and Vidyapati but what gave an upper hand to Coleridge was his trust on his imagination. This trust was deeply rooted in him and he often thought that the shape of life is given through imagination. In his poem *Dejection* he has tried to explain that imagination is a kind of nature which acts like a faithful companion to all the living beings. It lives inside a normal human being and from there it creates several external images. These images play a very vital role in understanding the values of life. Thus Coleridge always considered imagination as a superior form to all the living forces. Few lines from the poem can make us understand his views which matters a lot to him. It needs our attention when he writes-

> "Ah! From the soul itself must issue forth
> A light, a glory, a fair luminous cloud
> Enveloping the Earth-
> And from the soul itself must there be sent
> A sweet and potent voice, of its own birth,
> Of all sweet sounds the life and element!"[5]

It is very unusual to quote Vidyapati and Coleridge together as they hardly have any form of comparison but their stylistic features are striking and noteworthy. I have tried to measure the brightness of imagination associated with Vidyapati with the fair luminous cloud of imagination associated with Coleridge. Both are the poems of different genres but it looks that somewhere they think alike. Their style of writing is also different yet there is a match between their school of thoughts and in this regard Vidyapati exceeds the limits of Coleridge. It is a fact that Coleridge does not think so far as Vidyapati in the claims which he shows for fanciful imagination. He gets hampered by the external world and the balance between the internal and external form of nature is broken. His imagination is shapeless and thus his use of symbols and images are also not concrete. It is a kind of shapeless creation. There are other comparisons also but they are not worthy enough to be mentioned here because this chapter is dedicated to style and features only. In terms of intonation we can see that Vidyapati has successfully written his poems which can be sung beautifully as there is a kind of proper rhythm and pattern in his poems. He hesitates to write the free verse and he has discovered his own style of writing which is certainly unique but still inspiring. He begets his inspiration from God and it proves that he is far better than almost all of his contemporaries. The devotional songs of Krishna and Radha are still today celebrated and sung. It seems that these songs and poems are new and fresh. Every time when we read the poems of Vidyapati we find something new as there are numerous references to Indian mythology and philosophy. They are not only philosophy but they present the stark reality of life. These realities are not applicable to only a particular place but they are universal in appeal as well as tone. They are the rare collections of Indian tradition and culture. Apart from these facts we can also notice some linguistic peculiarities in the writings of Vidyapati. In most of his poems and songs third person narrative form has been used. We can find third person verbal form in several other poems of Maithili Literature. It shows that poets are literary genius and they have very special kind of knowledge. It is one of the reasons that they are known as the creators. Shelley has written in his *Defense of Poetry* that poets are not common and their knowledge is really praiseworthy. He has tried to convince that —

> "He not only beholds intensely the present as it is, and discovers those laws according to which present things ought to be ordered, but he beholds the future in the present, and his thoughts are the germs of the flower and the fruit of latest time... A poet participates in the eternal, the infinite, and the one,"[6]

Shelley considered a poet as a seer who has a peculiar insight and thus he is a kind of gift to the world. It is the nature of reality that gifted minds have peculiar insight as well as habits. A normal man cannot perceive the world like a poet and it does not mean that poets are not normal. They have something very special to them. Shelley has used the theory of knowledge given by Plato and he has applied it to the beautiful mind of a poet. This concept of Shelley is equally applicable to poets like Vidyapati. Shelley and Vidyapati have nothing to do with each other. They both belong to different ages yet the poems written by Vidyapati prove that he was a creator. The theory of Shelley is applicable to all the poets who are acting like a source of inspiration for the coming generation. It is the beautiful mind of a poet which gives life to images and symbols through the use of his creativity. We have talked about the use of diction by Vidyapati. It is a kind of tool which has been used by Vidyapati in his poems. It is derived from the past participle form of archaic transitive verbs. It also justifies the gender used in the poetry. It was a popular mode of writing because several popular poets have used this form extensively in their writings. The adverbial forms of the poems dedicated to spirituality have also been used by the poets like Vidyapati. It is one of the reasons that songs of Krishna and Radha got popularity in almost all the parts of India. Although Vidyapati has been admired by different critics and scholars but Pandit Janaki Vallabh Shastrijee has a different view point. He says that Vidyapati has written different poems on Radha and Krishna but in all of his poems he has depicted Radha in terms of beauty and desire. Radha as depicted by Vidyapati is a figure of Vasna or desire but in the poems of Surdasa the same Radha acts like an epitome of firmness. Now, we have two forms of Radha one is beautiful but weak but the other is not ugly but strong. Thus there is a view point that beauty is associated with weakness. A lady who is beautiful and submissive is weak or we can say that she is considered as the weaker section of the society. As far as I think, Vidyapati has no doubt portrayed Radha as a beautiful lady but no where it is refereed that she is weak. She is soft but not weak. She is submissive but it does not mean that she is weak. We are studying about the love poems of Vidyapati and British poets and we have seen the approach of Petrarch towards beauty. In the writings of Petrarch and in the theories of Platonic love, we have seen that a lady or the beloved has been depicted as beautiful and submissive but she is strong enough to make her lover persuade her. In the poems of Sidney and Spenser, we have seen that a beloved is beautiful enough to be treated as a kind of guiding star by her lover. The lover blindly follows her and it does not mean that she is weak. It is all about love and one needs to be submissive in love so that the other partner can remain active with her. If both the lover and the beloved will be active in love then the relationship is not going to last forever. Pandit Janaki Vallabh Shastrijee has tried to compare the beauty associated with Radha to the kind of firmness projected by Surdasa . In Vidyapati, we can find Radha as a kind of girl who is soft spoken. Surdasa has a different approach to beauty which is not soft but firm. The combination of softness and firmness cannot assure a healthy relationship. It is one of the reasons that Vidyapati has associated beauty with softness, which must be handled with care. In the poems of John Donne, we can also see that the beloved or the lady is beautiful and submissive. The lover feels complete in the presence of his beloved, and, it is equally applicable to the beloved also. We cannot deny that Vidyapati is a sensual poet who has associated beauty with desire but we cannot affirm that the beautiful beloved is weak. These facts are also associated with imagination. The poet tries to mix reality with imagination. Sex and gender is associated with society, and, both these terms are not alike. There is power associated with sex and gender. This power politics affirms that sex is determined biologically but gender is constructed by the society. This is one of the reasons that there are several individuals who are male, but, they behave like a female. This is also applicable to females who behave like a male in a particular society. This can be one of the reasons that Spartan women are considered equal to the men because they have trained like that, from their childhood.

Thus, it is proved that gender is a kind of tool which is created and sharpened by the society. There can be a lot of reasons that why do some male and female act opposite to their sexes in the society. It can be an effect of naturalism because according to the naturalistic philosophy, identity of any individual is an outcome of heredity and environment. A child generates and adopts the symptoms of any society. His upbringing is responsible for his particular behavior. It is our assumption that a girl child is beautiful and weak. In the case of Surdasa, there is firmness associated with Radha because he has tried to present Radha as firm and strong. His imagination is compact and he associates Radha with Shakti. In case of Vidyapati, we see Radha as beautiful as she should be seen in any normal society. Her friends are like her comrades but it is also noticeable that her friends are also females not males. These friends should also be beautiful and submissive as they are females, but, they act as comrades of Radha. It means that they are allowed to gaze the masculine beauty associated with the lover of Radha. If they can handle the masculine attention then why cannot Radha herself do it? The answer of this question lies in Indian culture and tradition where a lady feels too shy to look at her lover in public. It does not mean that she is weak, but, she is feeling shy at the presence of her lover. This kind of shyness does not hint that she is submissive, but it can be seen as a kind of response towards her lover. She is reciprocating the love of her lover through her shyness. It is the beauty of Vidyapati that he understands the minute observations of a lover and his beloved. He wants to capture the flux of emotions related to love in his poetry. The shyness of Radha is a kind of enjoyment which can be understood by her body language and can be figured out by reading the beautiful poems of

Vidyapati. This kind of experience is not common. William Blake is the other Romantic Poet who has captured the image of a man passing through the phases of innocence to experience. In *The Four Zoas* he says that-

> "What is the price of experience? Do men buy it for a song?
> Or wisdom for a dance in the street? No, it is bought with price
> of all that a man hath, his house, his wife, his children. Wisdom is sold in the desolate market where none come to buy,
> and in the wither'd field where the farmer plows for bread in vain."[7]

Blake was very much aware that experience cannot be gained easily. It is often bitter to find the reality associated with experience because it can be acquired only by paying a heavy price. For poets like Vidyapati, innocence and experience matters a lot. The beloved or the lady portrayed in his poem is very beautiful and submissive, but, we cannot say that she is innocent. She is aware of all the things around her. Knowingly or unknowingly, she also likes the admirer of her beauty. In case of William Blake, the experience is bitter because according to his thought and philosophy, experience can be attained at the cost of innocence but in case of Vidyapati, it seems that experience and innocence plays together. Even the poet is very much aware about this fact. He has written several poems on several themes but his love poems affirm it. The divinity associated with love has both the things- innocence as well as experience yoked together. The comrades of Radha are getting experience of love when they tell their friend that her lover is very handsome. They are gaining experience, but they are not innocent. Even Radha is not innocent and it does not mean that her experience is bitter. Each and every time, experience cannot be bitter. In the love poems of Vidyapati, we can find sensuality as he talks about the beauty associated with female body. He praises the beauty associated with the female breasts, tender lips, and slender waist and there is nothing immoral in it. As far as I think, love is never blind. It is not correct when we often say that love is blind, but it really does not mean that blind people cannot love. It can be said that in love a man can turn blind and he can be easily deceived by his beloved. It is equally applicable to the beloved also and she can also be deceived in love. Love is not blind, but the circumstances of love can make the lover as well the beloved blind so that they both can deceive each other. It happens because a circle of trust is created between the lover and his beloved. This circle of trust can be broken and the feeling is very painful. In Virah-Vedna, when a lover and a beloved is far away from each other then this circle of trust keeps their love safe and secure. It can be broken if either the lover or the beloved thinks that he or she is getting cheated in love. The situation can be created also by some foes of love but Vidyapati has written that the intensity of love increases in Virah-Vedna. The lover and the beloved enjoy the situation yet there is pain and anguish associated with Virah-Vedna. Thus, there is pleasure as well as pain in love. Pleasure is the memory of the lover and the beloved. Both of them keep on thinking about the good time which they have spent together. Their love is blind as they both trust each other very much. Initially, when a boy stare a girl with love, then he is wounded by the cupid's dart. Several scholars have accepted that love is not blind but in some cases we cannot be sure as there can be different circumstances leading to love. Vidyapati has written poems on it. It means that love cannot be kept under the songs of innocence or experience. It is a feeling which is divine, and divinity is purity. Sometimes purity is associated with innocence but we cannot say that every time experience is bitter. The concept of love related to the poets like Matthew Arnold is more experienced but it does not mean that it is not divine. Metaphysical poets always consider love as divine and pure. We have seen Arnold's and John Donne's concept of love. Donne considers sex as a medium to attain divinity. A soul can identify and love the other soul only through the body. The love of a lover and a beloved is incomplete without sex. They do not believe in Platonic concept of love and so believe that the art of sex can carry the lover and the beloved in the realms of spirituality. It is to be noticed that when William Blake talks about innocence and experience, he relates the innocent with childhood and experienced with adulthood. We cannot associate it with the innocent and experienced state of love. It is also right that love happens and if experience is the last stage of love then innocence must be the first or initial stage of love. Platonic love and metaphysical love can be two wings associated with the innocent and experienced stages of love. Another poet, who uses similar kind of images and symbols as used by Vidyapati is Thomas Wyatt. It is a truth that he has been neglected for so many years but in recent days his reputation as a good poet has been restored. His lighter lyrics are the master pieces of Sixteenth Century. The pure diction, attractive rhythm, is parallel to Vidyapati and it is one of the reasons that in recent days it appeals to the taste of a modern reader. It is often said about Thomas Wyatt that he is the one who has done the first experiment with the form of English Sonnets. In reality, he is the poet who acts as a role model for Elizabethan Poetry. Dr. Tillyard has taken an apology for the sonnets and he remarks that –

"For the sake of his reputation, Wyatt had better not have imported the sonnet into England, for by so doing he purchased a text-book glory at the price of advertising the class of poems that does his poetical powers least credit."[8]

Tillyard says that the sonnets of Wyatt need more considerations because he really deserves it. It cannot be taken as for granted because they are the "poems in their own right, and not merely as historically important bores."[9] However different scholars have also agreed that there are not many comparisons between Vidyapati and Wyatt. I have found some images, symbols and certain styles common in them. Wyatt follows the Italian parameters for composing poems where as Vidyapati is a typical Indian Poet bounded by Indian tradition and culture. Coming back to the view points of Janaki Vallabh Shastrijee, we will find that he has presented another view point regarding the writings of Vidyapati and Jaydev. Shastrijee has tried to show us that Vidyapati was influenced by Jaydev. Both Jaydev and Vidyapati write on similar subject matter. It is none of our business to present a comparison between Vidyapati and Jaydev but it is also right that there are various similarities between these two poets. The lyricism associated with the poems of Vidyapati and Jaydev looks alike but in case of Vidyapati there is no uniformity as he has a lot of varieties to write upon. These varieties are unique in itself. As for example, if we go to read the devotional poems of

Radha and Krishna we can feel that we are also reading a love poem. We think that love is also a kind of spirituality or a way to attain the divinity. At the same time, we are reminded about the Metaphysical Poets like John Donne. He has also said that by love or through love we can feel the spirituality associated with love. Matthew Arnold has also written that a lover and his beloved should not waste their time in thinking and they should grab the opportunity to love each other. By loving each other, they can feel spiritual power inside them. If we try to analyze the stylistic features of Vidyapati, we can see that in the translated poems done by Sri Aurobindo the maximum songs have a typical rhyme scheme which is lyrical in nature. There are so many poems in English literature which have similar rhyme scheme. It was also found in the sonnets of Shakespeare. If we try to analyze further the writing style of Vidyapati in terms of symbols and images used by him then it is not an easy task. There are a lot of symbols and images used by Vidyapati in his poems and songs. In Pranay-Duti of Vidyapati we can find that a loyal lover has been compared to the elements like gold. The comrades cum friends of Radha are preaching her that in this world it is too tough to find a true lover. It is also applicable to the modern period and that is why it has often been refereed that the songs and poems of Vidyapati are universal in nature. The friends of Radha are suggesting her that a loyal lover is like the element of gold. They are also telling her that before falling in love we must judge our own heart and thus we should be loyal in love. So there must be a proper mutual understanding in love. Gold has some special features as apart from its brightness it is also less reactive. A lot of heat is required to melt the gold and thus a lover who is true to his beloved is less reactive to the beauty of other girls and thus it is needless to say that he will be loyal to his beloved for his entire life. Such lovers are full of values and anything can be sacrificed to gain the hand of such lover. It is also true that such lovers are rarely found. Friends of Radha are teaching her the lessons of love as if they are the true masters of love. Here English Poets differ from Vidyapati in terms of content. There is uniformity of content in British Poets and it seems that they lack in producing varieties. Vidyapati is a kind of poet who is best known for his variety of contents. In Virah-Vedna, the friends or the messengers of Radha visits Lord Krishna and says that Radha is missing him. She is feeling so lonely that she may die. She is feeling wounded by the dart of Cupid, and thus, she cannot even imagine to live without her lover. It seems that she has not seen her lover from several years. Sexual gratification is the vehicle of love. It is not only an act but it acts like a medium to explore the divinity and spirituality associated with love. The following lines from *The Sunne Rising* will make the point crystal clear where John Donne says that-

> "She is all states, and all princes, I,
> Nothing else is.
> Prices doe but play; compar'd to this,
> All honour's mimique; all wealth alchimie."[10]

The lover feels complete with his beloved and thinks that in mutual love he himself is one of the greatest king or ruler of this world. This feeling of superiority comes to him when he is present with his beloved. If he would have been alone then he could have never thought that he is the ruler of the world. It means that his beloved empowers him. In opposite to this in Virah-Vedna of Vidyapati, Radha is feeling secluded as her lover is very far away from her. She is feeling pain in separation and this pain is so strong that she acknowledges that she cannot live without her lover. This picture of the beloved is very emotional and Vidyapati has beautifully presented the sentiment of the beloved. Jaydev has written similar kind of poetry in *Geetgovindam*. Coming back to the role of symbols and images in the poems of Vidyapati, we can find that beauty of Radha has been compared to the beauty of the moon. In songs of separation, Radha is feeling the anguish of love and it cannot be relieved even by the moon Goddess. This kind of image reflects the thought of the poet. The image of moon stands for beauty and coldness. Coldness is associated with death and it means that Vidyapati can project an image of multiple meaning at different situation. From time to time, the role of images keeps on changing. In the poems of "Kamopadesh" [11] we can find the code of conduct of a beloved. Radha is being taught by her friends that how she should carry herself while going to meet her lover. Her friends are telling her that she should look beautiful to Krishna. She must prepare herself for this meeting, and from head to toe, she should be decorated with all the feminine charms so that her lover can notice her each and every moves and curves. The lover should feel the excitement to love you and you must not show him any of your feminine charms so that the excitement should reach at its climax. By doing this the lover will be compelled to plead to his beloved to have mercy on him. In return she must not submit herself to him. She should feel the shyness associated with love and by doing so she can captivate her lover in her eyes. These are the tips given to Radha by her friends and she listens to such preaching calmly. By agreeing upon these teachings she can be sure that the relationship will always be beautiful where she can have a leading role in love. By reading this form of poetry, we are reminded about the courtly love culture which flourished during the middle ages. In the courtly love culture the beloved is always treated by her lover as his master. There is a kind of master-slave relationship between the lover and the beloved. The lover belongs to a high class society, yet he treats his beloved as his Goddess and he himself as her devotee. She is followed by her lover everywhere. In Vidyapati, we cannot find any courtly love culture yet we can have some glimpse of it as the beloved longs for an upper hand in the relationship. By reading such a beautiful poem of Vidyapati, we can feel that Cupid himself has come to train Radha that how should she act in front of her lover. Her friends are expert in training her and they are telling Radha that she must not express her love to the lover but she should listen to her lover silently. Whenever her lover tries to touch her she must not submit herself to him but she should give her refusal at the first touch. She should hide her breasts so well that the lover can get half glimpse of it and she should remain doing it until the last phase of her shyness. This form of poetry has been charged by different critics as erotic but there are also so many scholars who praise such form of writings. Approaching to the later poems of "Madhu-Milan"[12] we can find that the beloved is going to the house of her lover. This is her first visit and she is feeling scared. The tears are falling down to the earth but these tears are the tears of happiness. Vidyapati writes that the pleasure of love comes from the pain as the first night is going to be painful both for the lover as well as the beloved. The lover is also excited but his excitement is hidden. In these poems, it seems that Vidyapati is imitating the real life situations of a lover and his beloved. The readers can feel the sentiments hidden in such imitations. It is the positive effect of imitation that it pleases the readers up to a great extent so that Sidney says-

> "Poetry therefore is an arte of imitation, for so Aristotle termeth it in the word mimesis, that is to say, a representing, counterfeiting, or figuring foorth- to speake metaphorically, a speaking picture: with this end, to teach and delight."[13]

It is the style of Vidyapati that he imitates the crude form of human nature. He has a kind of understanding and insight which is very uncommon in any poets of Maithili Literature. To Sidney, the purpose of poetry lies in the fact that it should generate certain effects in the mind of the readers and according to him good poets are the poets who-

> "Imitate both to delight and teach, and delight to move men to take that goodness in hande, which without delight they would flye as from a stranger."[14]

Here a question arises that Vidyapati imitates different circumstances of life but in his poetry, can we find delight and teaching mixed together? It is a very simple question because certainly there is a lot of amusement and delight in his poetry but we cannot be sure about teachings. In his devotional songs we can find that as a reader we too get involved personally in almost all of his poems. There can be some teachings in his poetry that is why he is considered as a source of inspiration not only for poets but for readers also. We are greatly moved by reading poems on Shakti, Radha and Krishna and many others. We have also seen that the marriage song of Vidyapati is so dynamic that it always looks fresh. Grierson has rightly said about Vidyapati that his songs and poems will always be celebrated.

NOTES AND REFERENCES

1. E.K.Chambers & F.Sidgwick, *Early English Lyrics*, Sidgwick & Jackson publishers, London, 1937.p.1

2. www.john-keats.com/gedichte/endymion_i.htm

3. https://www.aurobindo.ru/workings/sa/08/0155_e.htm

4. These lines are taken from the letters of Samuel Taylor Coleridge,2,450.

5. https://www.poetryfoundation.org/poems/43973/dejection-an-ode

6. These lines are taken from the ed. version of Shelley's Defence of Poetry and it is translated by Harry Buxton Forman, London,1880

7. Blake, William, *The Four Zoas, Night The Second* in Poetry and prose.p.278

8. Tillyard, E.M.W, *The Poetry of Sir Thomas Wyatt*, Chatto & Windus publishers, London,1949.p.6

9. It is a phrase which has been taken from the articles of Hallett Smith entitled The Art of Sir Thomas Wyatt, The hunting library quarterly from August 1946. It acts like a mile stone in the appreciations of the sonnets of Wyatt.

10. Malaviya & Rizvi, *Donne and his Selected Poems*, Student Stores, Bareilly,1995.p.88

11. Poetry composition of Vidyapati under the title Kamopadesh meant his love poems and the title reflects sensuality associated in the love poems.

12. Madhu-Milan is the collection of poems written by Vidyapati. Here the first meeting of a lover and his beloved is shown by the poet.

13. Sidney, Philip, *An Apology for Poetry*, Elizabethan critical essay, ed. G. Gregory Smith, London,1904,p.158

14. Ibid,p.159

****

Chapter Four

Vidyapati and British Poets

As the title of the work suggests, it is an attempt to provide some fresh exposition of similarities and dissimilarities in the works of Vidyapati and British Poets. We know that Vidyapati is a kind of poet who has written poems on various subjects, but, in this chapter, I shall focus on the love poems written by Vidyapati and some British Poets. Love is a subject which has been talked about by different poets in different ages. In the works of Vidyapati, we can see the traditional Indian moral thoughts, which are hard to find in British Poets. Love is a kind of emotion which is very private in nature and it has always been associated with morality. There are also some issues related to the concepts of morality because what is considered immoral in one society, can be considered as moral in other one. This is one of the major reasons that some poets flourished well in their age, because they wrote according to the demand of time. Plato always considered poets unfit for the society especially, love poets. According to him, these poets detached themselves from the reality. He was of the view that poets were imitating nature and imitation cannot be a reality. By reading love poems, the young generation or the coming generation can become weaker and weaker. There is no place left in the society for the weaker emotions. Thus, love poets as well as the love poems were not approved by him. Later on, the concept of Plato was not approved and it was realized that imitation was not always bad but it can be fruitful also. In the works of Vidyapati and almost all the British Poets, we can see that the different sources of nature have been imitated. Vidyapati has several collections of poetry credited to his name and few important ones are *Nachari, Preeti Prasang, Vipralabdha, virah vedna* and many others. In these collections, we can find different elements of love and devotion coming together. In *Virahvedna*, the loneliness of a lover and his beloved has been talked about. Both the lover and the beloved are separated and this separation is providing them a kind of pain which is difficult to express. The beloved longs for her lover and sings various songs but the lover cannot respond back, because he is very far away from her. Such kind of poems has also been written by various British Poets, especially, the Romantic writers. The collections, like Vipralabdha, are also very precious because here, we can find the most valued philosophies of the poet. He was a kind of poet who was considered as an artistic genius. His poems are easy to understand because most of them are related to basic human existence and love. It has already been said that Vidyapati wrote in Maithili language which is most prevalent in North Bihar of India. He has also been claimed as a Bengali writer by different scholars because there are linguistic similarities between Maithili and Bengali. His songs of Krishna and Radha are very popular and it has crossed several boundaries. It is one of the prime reasons that his poems have been translated in different languages. Even Rabindra Nath Tagore has tried to copy the style of Vidyapati in his writings. Sri Aurobindo has translated the poems of Vidyapati in English after returning from England. In one of the songs of Vidyapati, translated by Sri Aurobindo, we can see the creativity of the poet. The lines of the song are as follows-

> "Playing she plays not, so newly shy,
> She may not brook the passing eye.
> Looking she looks not lest surmise
> Laugh from her own girl - comrades' eyes.
> Hearken, o hearken, Madhav to me.
> Just is the case I bring to thee.
> Radha today these eyes beheld;
> A maid she is unparalleled…"[1]

The above lines clearly show that Vidyapati was really a great poet who was able to think something very different from his contemporaries. He successfully portrays the image of a girl who is very beautiful and her friends are referred as her comrades. Such kind of writings can be seen in the poets who tried to follow the Petrarchan style of writing. In Petrarchan sonnets we have seen that the beloved was considered as very beautiful who can never be paralleled by any other maid. It was also the spirit of Renaissance Poets who usually wrote in such a fashion. In describing the beauty of a girl or the beloved there is an extended use of simile and metaphor. Sometimes the beloved is compared to the moon or the redness of her lip is compared with the red flowers like Rose. In the above poem the gaze of the girl has been beautifully presented by the poet. She is playing yet not playing or we can say, she is watching or yet not watching. Only her lover can understand the language of her eyes which is presented through her friends who have been referred as comrades. Such kind of writings can also be seen in the poets of Elizabethan Period. Edmund Spenser has written the poem *Amoretti* in the Sixteenth Century. In this poem, his courtship with Elizabeth Boyle has been described. It is a sonnet cycle which describes the pangs of a lover. This kind of Poetry has been introduced in England by Sir Thomas Wyatt, who has borrowed it from France. *Amoretti* was criticized by several critics and scholars but it has some good qualities also. In comparison to *Amoretti*, his *Epithalamion* was considered more praiseworthy. It was written for his bride and it was a kind of marriage song. It is very interesting to see that Vidyapati has also written marriage songs. The songs written by Vidyapati and Spenser differ in tone. In Spenser, we can find that the groom is impatient as it seems to him that the time is not passing, but it has ceased itself. The lover is fastened and he is unable to control himself. The poet has tried to write about the anxiousness of the lover and he is unable to wait for the marriage rituals. It looks so realistic as if it is happening in the real life of a lover. The common element between these two poets is sensuality. Vidyapati focused more on the beauty of the beloved and writes-

> "Ah, who has built this girl of nectarous face?
> Ah, who this matchless, beauteous dove?
> An omen and a bounteous boon of love,
> A garland of triumphant grace [2]."

The above lines clearly hint about the poet's approach to beauty. He is trying to thank the almighty who has made such a beautiful maid. Spenser too writes about the beauty of the girl but his creation is full of unusual images and symbols. Such kind of comparison is missing in the poetry of poets like William Shakespeare. He is a kind of poet who hardly writes about female beauty. He is concerned more about the male beauty. In his poems, we can find several unusual things. There is a kind of conflict between ethical inhibitions and love in his sonnets. The conflict can be seen only in few poems of Shakespeare, and thus, it is not applicable to all of his sonnets. When I say that there is a conflict between ethical inhibitions and love, I mean to say that there is a kind of constraint or hurdle in his concept of love. The hurdle has been created by the social code of conduct which is associated with morality. The society is not ready to accept such kind of relationships. Although, the society is changing a lot in the modern period, but, we need to keep patience and courage to understand the clear distinction between morality and immorality. Such a kind of relationship is not considered as natural, as it is developed by an insight which is considered as a kind of disorder. This disorder leads to homosexuality which is considered as immoral in society. When a person violates the code of conduct of any society then he becomes a kind of subject who will have to experience the pangs of his own society. It generally happens because of the desire of a man or a woman who often goes against the moral order. In case of a sensitive person, this kind of experience is very painful. People who are generally unscrupulous or whose mind has been hardened by his own thought, violate this code of conduct. They take decisions directly from their heart and never think that it can be a punishable offense. It is also correct that it happens only with a few people because majority of them take decisions from their own mind. There is always a sense of dualism between reason and passion, mind and heart, body and soul. In these cases, most of the times, a sensitive person fails to decide that what is right and what is wrong. William Shakespeare is a kind of poet who often admires his male friend in his poems. Critics and several scholars have charged him with unnatural perception of love. He is often talked and discussed by scholars that what can be the type of relationship between a man and other man? Is it natural or unnatural? It is a kind of sexual attachment and the poet has himself accepted that he longs for his friend. In sonnet number Eighteen he writes –

> "Shall I compare thee to a summer's day?
> Thou art more lovely and more temperate:
> Rough winds do shake the darling buds of May,
> And summer's lease hath all too short a date."[3]

Above lines clearly says that how deeply the poet is in love with his friend. We are not sure about the assumption that this kind of love actually depicts the theme of homosexuality but critics and several scholars have charged Shakespeare for this. The beauty of the friend of Shakespeare is lovelier than the summer's day. The poet has idealized or glorified his relationship with his friend. Generally, we have seen that in a relationship, a lover praises his beloved, but here, who is the lover and who is the beloved, is not known. It is not normal as the poet has idealized his concept of love. He is very brave because he has brought forward the hidden relationships of a private life into the public. It needs a lot of courage because in a civilized society there are so many things which are occurring and we are totally unknown to such kind of changes. Shakespeare says that he has committed certain faults with his friend. He and his friend both of them are sinners and he is feeling guilty for such faults, but he finds himself helpless. In his poems, the language is easy to understand, but the same language also speaks that the poet is biased and he is trying to defend his friend. They both are sinners which he himself has accepted but he finds himself responsible for it. Both are sinners because both are sensual. It might also reflect that both of them have sexual affairs with different kind of women. Shakespeare wants that his friend must be excused because he loves him. Some sonnets also convey the message that he wants his friend not to be excused because if he is to be punished then he wants his friend to accompany him. Even in hell he does not want to be separated from his friend. If he gets the company of his friend in hell then that hell will also become a kind of heaven. It reflects the fact that Shakespeare is a kind of person who is scared of loneliness and he does not want to be left alone. He hates rejection in life. In Sonnet number thirty six, the poet writes that-

"let me confess that we two must be twain,
Although our undivided loves are one:
So shall those blots that do with me remain,
Without thy help, by me be borne alone.
In our two loves there is but one respect,
though in our lives a separable spite,
which though it alter not love's sole effect...."[4]

The poet feels that there is a kind of rift between him and his lovely friend. At the same moment, he also understands that he cannot live happily without his friend. Both of them are inseparable. His friend is the Earl of Southampton and for the rift between him and his friend he blames himself. Shakespeare has a different perspective to think and analyze the situations in which he is trapped with his friend. He finds himself guiltier than his friend, although they both are equally guilty of the sin which they have committed altogether. I have given a detailed description of Shakespeare and his friend because such kind of things has also been written by poets like Vidyapati. He also talks about male bonding. There are references to poems in which he has written about his patron, whom he treated as a close friend. There are few critics and scholars who have also charged Vidyapati for having a good and fondly relationship with his friend. We have seen in the part of Introduction that Vidyapati was closely associated with the rulers of Oinwar dynasty. He was also inspired by the courtly culture of the dynasty. Maharaj Shiv Singh was a close friend of the poet and he was always favoured by the king. The poet was only two years older than the king. There are several instances where both of them shared good time with each other. Vidyapati has written numerous poems for his friend and his queen, Lakhima Devi. Maharaj Shiv Singh was one of the greatest admirers of Vidyapati. There is an instance, when the Sultan of Delhi has captivated Shiv Singh when he was a prince. Vidyapati became restless after getting this news that his friend has been captivated by the Sultan of Delhi. He himself went to Delhi and tried to persuade the Sultan of Delhi to release his friend from the prison. Sultan was amazed to see that Vidyapati was not a soldier or fighter who has come to challenge him, but a poet. He was greatly moved by this poet and after taking test of his poetry, he himself became one of the greatest admirers of Vidyapati. This was the greatness of this poet and Shiv

Singh was released immediately. This kind of friendship is not equal to the friendship of William Shakespeare and his friend. This is the greatness of love that there cannot be any comparison of love. Nobody can compare two true lovers and friends and say that someone is the best while other is worst. We are reminded that once Shakespeare has accepted that he and his friend, both are sinners but he his guiltier than his friend. He wants to safeguard the dignity of his friend as if it is his own dignity. Maharaj Shiv Singh and Vidyapati are also good friends and they are also not separable. Thus we can see that Vidyapati was a great poet as well as a great friend, who always trusted on his friendship. Shakespeare and Vidyapati are the two poets of different genres who were admired and respected in two different ages. Both of them have written on male bonding and love. Their poems are not easy to compare because both of them write in different styles. The themes, motifs and symbols can be similar but the style of writing is totally different. Vidyapati is platonic as well as an admirer of physical form of beauty whereas Shakespeare is more realistic. His philosophy of love is rarely found in any society. Readers can find similarities as well as differences between these two poets. Comparisons between these two poets are remarkable. The concept of beauty is also different for Shakespeare and in sonnet number one hundred and thirty, he says –

> "My mistress' eyes are nothing like the sun;
> Coral is far more red than her lips' red;
> If snow be white, why then her breasts are dun;
> If hairs be wires, black wires grow on her head.
> I have seen roses damasked, red and white,
> But no such roes see I in her cheeks;
> And in some perfumes is their more delight
> Than in the breath that from my mistress reeks..."[5]

The above lines reflect the reality that the poet is not going to give us false comparisons. There are several other things which are more beautiful than the beloved of the poet. The breasts of the beloved are not white but dun-colored and her hairs are like black wires. Shakespeare is a kind of poet who is giving us the true image of his beloved. We have seen that during the courtly love culture, a beloved was compared with several beautiful images like roses and moon. The lover always tried to follow his beloved because she was considered more superior than the lover in terms of beauty and virtue. Vidyapati has also written about the similar kind of beauty and he has tried to establish the notion that feminine beauty is superior than masculine beauty. In fact, beauty is a term which can be applied only to a female. Thus, we can see that Shakespeare breaks all the code of conduct related to feminine beauty. He is not feeling ashamed in disclosing the fact that his beloved is not so beautiful. In spite of this he is not going to stop loving her. He has no fake commitments. He considers his friend, the Earl of Southampton far more beautiful than his beloved. Shakespeare successfully establishes the notion that beauty lies in the eyes of the beholder. Beauty is a term which is very personal and subjective in nature. What is beautiful for Vidyapati cannot be equally beautiful for Shakespeare or the vice-versa. There are no personal grudges because both of them are not contemporary. Such kind of things can also be seen in the Romantic Poets like John Keats, Shelley, and Byron. Wordsworth is a bit different poet in comparison to other Romantic Poets because he writes in a more splendid way. In the Poems of Vidyapati we can see and feel beauty in the form of desire. One of the main subjects of the Romantic Poet is nature. Vidyapati has also written about various forms of nature. Linguistically, these poets are different but in appeal of senses there is a kind of similarity. Scholars have argued that Vidyapati is far more superior to the Romantic Poets because he has written more deeply on natural objects. He compares the beauty of a lady to the beauty of the nature. Even his devotional songs are beauteous because there also, we can find the fragrance of nature. The linguistic approach of a poet can be termed as scientific because a poet tries to choose the correct words for correct emotions in his poems. On the other hand the mythical approach of writing poetry is not scientific but it is a kind of humanist approach. R.H.Robins has said that –

> "A field where in linguistics and Psychology meets at the borders of their respective domains through chains of casual connections within human brains linking experiences with writing and reading....this interdisciplinary study is called Psycho-linguistics."[6]

The present work or chapter is entitled Vidyapati and British Poets and thus a comparison is needed to be established which is cross-cultural. These are linguistic differences between Vidyapati and British Poets. The theme and motif can be similar but the tone and diction depends upon the language which is wide spread. Vidyapati is more respected and followed in Mithila whereas British Poets are widely read and circulated. It does not mean that Vidyapati is not expressive. The problem lies in the translation literature. We cannot find the correct mood and expression of any poem if it is translated. In spite of all these hurdles, the present work is a kind of attempt to draw a correct comparison between Vidyapati and British Poets. It is very interesting to compare the use of images and symbols in different cultures and geographical boundaries. To extract meaning from a meaning is not an easy task. British Poets have used images and symbols which are more expressive but Vidyapati has used images and symbols which are highly decorated. This kind of decoration of images in a particular form of poem is not usually seen in any British Poet. There are numerous references in almost all the lines of poems written by Vidyapati Thakur. C.k.Ogden and I.A.Richards have written in *The Meaning of Meaning* that symbolism is a kind of study of human affairs and it is said-

> "Symbolism is the study of the part played inhuman affairs by language and symbols of all kinds, and especially of their influence on thought. It singles out for special inquiry the ways in which symbols help us and hinder us in reflection on things ... the direct relation of symbols records events and communicate facts ... words...mean nothing by themselves... between a thought and a symbol causal relations hold. When we speak , the symbolism we employ is caused partly by the reference we are making and partly by social and psychological factors, the purpose for which

we are making the reference, the proposed effect of our symbols on other persons, and our own attitude. When we hear what is said, the symbols both cause us to perform an act of reference and to assume an attitude which will according to circumstances, be more or less similar to the act and the attitude of the speaker..."[7]

If we analyze the poems of Vidyapati and Spenser, as well as Shakespeare on the basis of their symbolism we can find that they differ at certain levels. They use symbols of all kinds but all these poets are selective in nature. In the poems of Shakespeare, facts are communicated through symbols and images. In the poems of Vidyapati, images and symbols are nurtured so well that it can directly influence our senses. In the poems of Spenser, images and symbols convey a very beautiful atmosphere of both despair and delight. His marriage song looks so fresh that still today it looks new and fair. There is a proper relationship established between a thought and a symbol in the poems of Spenser, Vidyapati, Shakespeare and some other poets belonging to the Elizabethan age. In the Romantic period poets, like Shelley, Keats and Byron, uses a different kind of symbols where we can hardly find any inter connected ideas. Poems of Wordsworth, Coleridge can be personal as in their poems we can see some personal moments of despair. Even John Keats talks about different form of symbols and ideas which are associated with loss and sufferings. We have drawn certain parallel images of male bonding between Vidyapati and Shakespeare but there are certain differences too. In Vidyapati we can see certain glimpse of Indian tradition. This tradition gives an integrated and holistic approach towards Purusa or manliness. This approach stresses over a fact that Purusa and the society is related intrinsically. This society has a pre established notion which is known as the code of conduct. A man is bounded by certain rules and regulations in the society. There are different rules for a male as well a female. The male is not supposed to adopt the rules made for the female and it is equally applicable to the female also. From here, the problems related to sex and gender starts. Sex is determined biologically whereas gender is constructed through the society. Both sex and gender are not equal but they are two different things. In every individual, both masculine as well as feminine parts co-exist. Thus, all of us are in parts masculine as well as feminine. It is not tough to understand but it depends upon the situation. The feminine aspect related to any person makes him soft and creative whereas the masculine parts make him tough to cope with the adverse situations of life. There are some hard times when a female is compelled to act like a male. In our Indian society, there are a lot of examples for it, as for example, the queen of Jhansi. Rosalind in *As You like It* written by William Shakespeare can be a best example in English literature. Such acts are considered as heroic if performed by a female because in a patriarchal society, a female is considered as weak and if she performs such acts of bravery then it is considered as heroic. The situation becomes very opposite when it happens with a man he is not expected to behave like a female. In war, when a prince tried to cry like a female because he cannot see the violence and turbulence all around then it was declared that the prince is unfit for kingship. It is the harsh reality as a man is supposed to be stronger than a woman so that he can safeguard the weaker section of the society. Similar is the case with Shakespeare. He is supposed to write about love affair between a man and a woman and it is considered normal in any society. Sexual relationship between a man and a woman is natural and normal and the society is ready to accept it, because it has not been challenged. Relationship between a man and other man is condidered unnatural. It is interesting to see that in such relationship someone plays the role of a lover whereas the other plays the role of a beloved. So, in such unnatural relationship and affair, the role play of the lover and the beloved is natural but the balance of the society is at stake. It is because of this balance such relationship is dangerous in nature so it is not accepted by the society. However, in modern times people are trying to understand such situations so that the relationship can be legalized. In several societies, it is considered as a sin, and thus, such practices must be stopped. If such a kind of relationship spreads widely and regularly, then it can be a threat to the society. These approaches are logically correct but love is considered something which is not rational. It needs a heart to bestow love and it is one of the reasons that there is a continuous war between mind and the heart. Mind says something whereas the heart says some thing else opposite to the mind. Reason and passion are the two different poles which can never be united. They run parallel to each other. Love has a logic which can be understood only by a genuine lover. The understanding of the subject of love is also associated with cultural studies. In A Handbook of Literary Terms written by M.H.Abrams and Geoffrey Galt Harpham it is disclosed that-

> "cultural studies designates a recent and rapidly growing cross-disciplinary enterprise for analyzing the conditions that affect the production, reception and

cultural significance of all types of institutions, practices and products; among these, literature is accounted as merely one of many forms of cultural practices. A chief concern is to specify the functioning of the social, economic and political forces and power structures that are said to produce the diverse forms of cultural phenomena and to endow them with their social meanings...."[8]

The above lines clearly reveal that cultural study is a cross-disciplinary enterprise. The present chapter Vidyapati and British Poets is also inter-disciplinary which has a direct link to the cultural studies. We can see a clear glimpse of Indian society in the poems of Vidyapati. In every society, there are certain similarities and in the subject like love traditions there are a lot of similarities between the poems of Vidyapati and some British poets. We have already seen male bonding and cross cultural love affairs which are capable to change any society. This change can be positive as well as negative, but, with the advancement of time the concept of a modern man and a modern society has also changed drastically. In *Puruspariksha*, Vidyapati has written about the behavior of a man which a society expects from him. One of the most prominent objectives of purusa is kama which means love. In purusa, there is an endowment of Rasa or emotion. It is a kind of feeling which is permanent. The purusa is also a person who has been affected by sentiments, can be of different types and the most divine form of purusa is of a lover. It is interesting to see that Vidyapati has classified such form of purusa into five different categories. First one is "anukula"[9] who is a faithful lover. His love for his beloved is genuine. This kind of lover is virtuous but impatient. We can say that he is a one woman man, who loves only his wife. He cannot think of any relationship beyond his marriage, and thus, any extramarital relationship is a kind of sin for such lovers. This is one of the reasons that he is virtuous and accomplished. His love for his wife is emotional as well as physical, thus, it is like bliss both for the lover and his wife. He also shows respect for his beloved because he loves her more than his own life. He cares for her a lot and if time will decay her beauty then also he is not going to stop loving her. It has mentioned that he loves her physically as well as emotionally so if her physical beauty will be withered away by any means, then also, he will stand for her forever. This kind of relationship is rarely seen and it is considered as pure and divine. Thus, his love is ageless and he is a kind of lover whose love can be felt by a beloved "in wealth, in tribulation, or even in death ne'er deserted she her lord. It is due to virtuous acts done in some former birth that a husband's love for such a wife is born."[10] such kind of lovers can also be seen in British Poems. There are few poets like Spenser, who has written poems on true love and "marriage"[11] we have already studied about Petrarchan Sonnets, where a lover is supposed to be a true lover and he blindly follows his beloved. Such kind of courtly love can be seen in Vidyapati when he talks about "Daksina"[12], who is a courteous lover. In spite of a wife, he has an affair with other woman. It is noteworthy to find that he presents his faithfulness to both his wife as well as his mistress whom he loves a lot. The character of this lover is doubtful yet he has been kept under the category of a real purusa. He is not a trustworthy lover as compared to the previous lover; yet, his features are praiseworthy because he is chivalric in nature. He has valour, intelligence and zeal contented within him. He is chief of the army and he has potential to handle any situation. He can die for his fellowmen. Such kind of poetry can be seen in chivalric romances. During the Restoration period such kinds of lovers were in fashion and culture. Sword and affair was considered as a matter of pride. In Indian culture as well as the English culture it was considered as a subject of immorality. Vidyapati has talked about such kind of lovers but he has stressed more on the morality which is necessary for any society to flourish. The only thing which is positive about such kind of lovers is their promise and valour. They can die for their promises and it has been witnessed that such lovers often fail because it becomes very tough to maintain a rhythmic balance between a wife and a mistress. Vidyapati terms a discerning lover as "Vidagdha".[13] He is an expert in the art of love making and it seems that he is born to love. By noticing such a lover, readers are bound to think about the sanctity of love where a professional lover is credible enough to be kept under the category of purusa. Vidyapati's meaning of purusa is not so easy to understand. It is a fact that such lovers are present in each and every strata of the society. Numerous poems have been written about their characteristic features. In Vidyapati and British Poets, there are several things to notice but the present research work is based upon the love traditions, so, we should try to follow only the love traditions which are present in Vidyapati and various British Poets. It is not necessary to unfold every sections of the poem in detail, but, the necessary topics must not be left behind. Vidyapati has also talked about a cozening rake that he terms as dhurta. He cannot love any woman and it is also true that no woman can love him but if any affair starts between the two, then it will be merely an eye wash. It will not be permanent and it will end soon. Thus, we can see that

Vidyapati was a poetic genius who left his contemporaries very far behind in every aspects. In reading the character sketch of a ghasmara[14], Vidyapati has successfully mentioned his nature. He is an infatuated lover who is witty but captive of his own sexual desires. He is so much infatuated in love that he forgets all other duties which needs to be performed essentially. He is not successful in love and he is betrayed by his own wife who ditches him for some jewels and pearls. This is so ill fated that the lover ruins his own life. Although, there are some poets in English who have written about infatuation but they have not given such a kind of detailed description where a lover ruins his own life in search of true love. There are some similarities between Vidyapati and metaphysical poets. There are poets like John Donne, Matthew Arnold and others who have written on love and there concept of love is physical as well as spiritual. Sexual and physical love is essential for spiritual gratification. John Donne advocates such a kind of relationship between a lover and his beloved where spirituality can be gained through sexuality. Sensuality is also related to Vidyapati and in his poems we can find detailed description of female beauty. John Donne is a great poet but even he cannot match the sensuality of Vidyapati. The technique of John Donne arises from his understanding of the ecstasy. In art of making love, it is not only the physical body of the lover and the beloved which gets united but even their souls are united. Vidyapati has said that love is so divine that we cannot separate the lover from his beloved. If the lover is separated from his beloved than he imagines that his separation is only of the body, not of the soul. Body as well as the soul plays an active role in love. Sexual relationship provides a way to find the soul entrapped in another soul which is very divine. Thus, divinity is a mental status which can be felt only through the body. Vidyapati as well as John Donne both of them have tried to make us understand that divinity and spirituality is not present outside the body but their way passes through the body. We cannot deny that they are right or wrong but we can expect a deeper and concrete idea of love by such a great poets. There are so many images and symbols which are used by love poets in their poems. These symbols and images are not erotic but adventurous. In *Amoretti* the context of the poem is as distinctive as the use of imagery. The technique used is allegorical in style. The exaggeration is calculated and the images used are emblematic. Such kinds of images are also present in the love poems of Vidyapati. There are several "myths"[15] created by Spenser in his poems. These myths are, not simply, an imagination based on real stories because they are self created and it can also be seen in Romantic writers. The Romantic writers combine the compactness of truth and imagination in such a way that it seems they have been inspired by any divine insight. For such a kind of insight Coleridge praises Wordsworth and says that-

> "it was the union of deep feeling with profound thought; the fine balance of truth in observing, with the imaginative faculty in modifying the objects observed; and above all the original gift of spreading the tone, the atmosphere, and with it the depth and height of the ideal world around forms, incidents, and situations, of which, for the common view, custom had bedimmed all the luster, had dried up the sparkle and the dew drops." [16]

Thus, it becomes clear that romantic writers always cared for spirit. They were concerned with the things of nature and they used their insight and imagination in understanding and presenting beautiful poems. It was a kind of quest or search for the world which was still unseen. Those emotions and inspirations were fresh and new and it was not general in appeal. For such a kind of emotion, William Blake has said that art is superior in nature but it deals with general truths. It is a kind of imagination which uncovers the real things. It will become clearer from the following lines-

"To see a world in a Grain of sand
And a heaven in a wild flower,
Hold infinity in the palm of your hand
And eternity is an hour."[17]

This kind of eternity is transcendental in nature. It is an insight of an inspiration which has been evoked out of the imagination. Such an imagination is very special. Thus, finally, we can say that Vidyapati and British Poets have written a lot of love poems and if we read the poems of Vidyapati then we will find that he is the real master of love poems, who has written varieties of love poems.

NOTES AND REFERENCES

1. Aurobindo, sri, *songs of Vidyapati*, Sri Aurobindo Ashram publishers, Pondicherry,1956.p.19
2. Ibid.p.28
3. www.shakespeare-online.com/sonnets/18detail.html
4. www.shakespeares-sonnets.com/sonnet/36

5. www.shakespeare-online.com/sonnets/130detail.html
6. R.H. Robins: *General Linguistic*, Longman Publishers, London, 1971.p.371
7. C.K. Ogden & I.A. Richards: The Meaning of Meaning, Trubner and Co. Ltd.London,1943.p.9
8. Abrams, M.H,*A Handbook of Literary Terms*, Boston: Wadsworth, 2009. p.64
9. Grierson, G.A, *The Test of A Man*,The Royal Asiatic Society, London, 1935.p.150
10. Marriage here means the songs of marriage written by Spenser
11. Special kind of lover mentioned in *Puruspariksha* written by Vidyapati
12. Ibid.
13. Ibid.
14. Ibid.
15. An admirable account of Spenser's treatment of allegorical myths is given in C.S.Lewis's *The Allegory of Love*, Chapter 7
16. https://books.google.co.in/books?isbn=0691018618
17. https://www.poetryfoundation.org/poems/43650/auguries-of-innocence

****

Chapter Five

Forms of Love

It has always been a tough task to define love. It is a kind of expression which varies from person to person. We have already seen and studied the Platonic form of love. We have noticed that purity and divinity is associated with the Platonic version of love. Poets like Vidyapati are often known as love poet. His concept of love is versatile and it is one of the reasons that he has been referred as a versatile genius by so many scholars. His love is not limited up to the relationship of a man with a woman. His poems on spirituality are also unique and he hardly talks about religion in spirituality. Relationship between a lover and his beloved has always been a very important section in the chapters associated with love. In this chapter I have tried to focus on almost all the important forms of love. We know that love has many faces and all the faces are dissimilar from each other. Basically there are four kinds of love and it has been affirmed by C.S.Lewis. he agrees that the four kinds of love exist in the world in the form of friendship, erotic, love of God and parents. This form of love encompasses all the kinds of problems and possibilities associated with love. There can be love between friends, children and parents, love of women for another women or men for men. Love between men and women are more classified. Above all can be love for God which is the ultimate source of happiness. It has been said earlier that it is very personal and the intensity of love changes or varies from person to person. In several forms of love which are stated above there can be several problems like the problems of possessiveness, sex, false sentimentality, pride, jealousy, or manners associated with love. When I say that even manners can be a problem in love, I mean to say that mixing private life in public life or the vice-versa can create problem in day to day life affairs. To be formal during intimate moments can never be a good choice. It is also truly applicable to the public life. One of the very basic questions associated with love is related to its existence. Love is a gift or need? It can be a gift of life as well as the need of life. We cannot expect a beautiful life without love. Several scholars have agreed to a point that love can be a gift if it leads our life towards progress. This progress is again a dynamic word which is very subjective in nature. Love for divinity is certainly a gift as it always gives us an insight to purify our soul as well as the body. In Plato's *Symposium* Socrates has recounted the doctrines of love. He says that these doctrines have been given to him by Diotima whom he considers as a wise woman. She affirms that love is evoked through beauty but the lover should accept it like stairs. It must travel from body to mind. Beauty is itself an idea or an image. It is not fixed but it keeps on changing. This is one of the reasons that love is never simple. Its understanding is very complex as it needs to be felt not to be understood. Beauty as an idea has the power to alienate the human soul. It seems that the human soul is in exile and there also the soul is searching for true love. The quest of true love is never fulfilled as love is a kind of idea which keeps on changing. This idea varies from person to person and it means that this world is full of unfulfilled love. This ideal beauty of the body and the mind revolves round the world and it is perceived through senses and thus it is far away from reality. It is distorted and distant and the reflections coming out of it is not permanent. Plotinus and different other Neo-Platonist have framed a new idea that all truth, goodness and beauty of the sensible world is a kind of radiation which is coming from the absolute power which we say God. Religious thinkers and scholars coming from the different sects of Christianity have affirmed that beauty and truth is God. Thus it is useful to quote the concept of a Platonic lover-

> "The Platonic lover is irresistibly attracted to the bodily beauty of a beloved person, but reverses it as a sign of the spiritual beauty that it shares with all other beautiful bodies, and at the same time regards it as merely the lowest rung on a ladder that leads up from sensual desire to the pure contemplation of Heavenly Beauty in God."[1]

This concept of Platonic love has been elaborated by different scholars and we can also find it in the writings of Petrarch, Dante and several other writers. It was a kind of fashion to write on the models of Platonic love during the age of renaissance. In *Amoretti*, Spenser has written on similar themes of love and beauty which needs to be understood. Few lines of the poem are very important in this regard as Spenser writes-

> "Men call you fayre, and you doe credit it....
> But only that is permanent and free
> From frayle corruption, that doth flesh ensew.
> That is true beautie: that doth argue you
> To be divine and borne of heavenly seed:
> Derived from that fayre spirit, from whom al true
> And perfect beauty did at first proceed."[2]

This doctrine of love is very philosophical and religious. The modern concept of Platonic love is a drastic misconception as it means that there should not be any sexual gratification in love. The Romantic Poets like Shelley was also fascinated by the concept of platonic love. It is also correct that in modern period, it has been misunderstood. Modern lover understands love but it is an irony that it cannot be understood. Modern concept of love stresses more on physicality "twice away from reality."[3] Similar to this we can say that love is not real but virtual. There are several forms of love which means that there is no fixed physical appearance of love. It is an abstract idea which is always expressed through feelings and emotions. These emotions are perceived by the sensory organs so sensation is often associated with love and affinity. The role of the poet is to provide shape to such abstract ideas. G.Wilson Knight refers to Theseus speech in Shakespeare's A Midsummer Night's dream. He says that a poet's pen should provide shape to the unknown things. His observations can be understood through the lines mentioned below-

> "... the source of poetry is rooted in the otherness of mental or spiritual realities; these, however, are a nothing until mated with earthly shapes. Creation is

thus born of a union between earth and heaven, the material and the spiritual."⁴

Thus, we can see that the role of a poet is very clear but it is a very tough task. Poets are successful in giving shapes to the unknown things but these shapes are not permanent. John Donne is a kind of poet who is known best for his metaphysical conceits. In his poems, we can find that the emotions like love are presented through the natural objects and different other images. In one of his poems entitled *The Flea*, Donne has written that the flea, an insect is not merely an insect but it should be treated like a temple. It is a kind of marriage bed as it contains the blood of both the lover as well as the beloved. Here, John Donne has tried to give shape to the abstract emotions like love. *The Flea* represents three lives as it contains blood of the three lives namely the lover, the beloved and the blood of itself. If a person is going to kill the flea, he is going to commit three crimes all together. This kind of farfetched imagery of John Donne is very famous as it is unique. John Donne observes that-

> "Mark but this flea, and mark in this,
> How little that which though deniest me is;
> It sucked me first, and now sucks thee,
> And in this flea our two bloods mingled be;
> Thou know'st that this cannot be said
> A sin, nor shame, nor loss of maidenhead."⁵

The above lines clearly show that during the time of John Donne loss of maidenhood was considered as a shameful act. The union of the lover and the beloved was considered as a sinful act, especially if it was performed before marriage. In *The Flea*, Donne has tried to search the possibilities of the lover and the beloved to get unified. *The Flea* becomes a temple or the marriage bed for the poet. This poem has appealed a lot to several scholars as it brings forward some mystic ideas of John Donne. Here a lover can notice a world of infinite within the finite. This kind of ability can be noticed in the Romantic poets like William Blake. He was a kind of poet who practiced to write the song of innocence as well as experience. In his *Auguries of Innocence* he has written that–

> "To see a world in a Grain of sand
> And a Heaven in a wild flower,
> Hold infinity in the palm of your hand
> And eternity in an hour."[6]

These opening lines of the poem presents the mystic ideas of William Blake and it parallels the mysticism associated with John Donne. It is very unusual to find such connections between two poets of different age and attitude. The current topic is so interesting that different writers, poets or authors can be compared irrespective of their age and attitude. Time and era has witnessed that love is life and life is mystic in nature. So we cannot deny the association of mysticism with love. It has also been mentioned by different scholars that this kind of mysticism emphasizes man's divinity which is innate. This is one of the greatest reasons that poets get inspired by the topics like love. Plato has also said in his *Ion* that poets are inspired by nature which reflects purity and divinity. Similar kind of purity and divinity can be seen in metaphysical poets. In the poems of John Donne, we can find the sexual association between the lover and his beloved. The poet think that it is a way to achieve divinity. While performing the act of love the individuality of the lover and the beloved is lost and they become one. This unification of the lover and the beloved provides a kind of satisfaction where body and soul becomes one. It is not less than finding the ultimate source of divinity. Different critics have charged poets like John Donne, Andrew Marvell as poets who cares only for physical pleasure. They are sensual in nature and they definitely do not care for morality. Love is a kind of subject which is divine and pure. The fact about divinity and purity is also not fixed. Purity and divinity associated with love is subjective in nature. It means that it varies from person to person. Romans believed that love cannot be purified without sex. In our Indian society, it is a taboo to write over such issues and topics. Sexuality without love means body without soul. Romans also believed that love and sex is closely associated with each other and they cannot be studied separately. As far as morality is concerned, it is also right, and so doing material business with any form of human emotions is always immoral. Love is the heightened form of human emotion and we can attain divinity by the power of love. John Donne and Andrew Marvell are such kind of poets who advocates for such kind of purity and divinity which needs to be understood. A layman cannot understand the metaphysical poetry of John Donne but he can feel it. This is not simply sensuality or something which can be refereed as immoral. To understand this few lines from the poem *The Extasie* needs to be quoted. In this poem John Donne writes about the real feelings of love. In this poem Donne has tried to say that real, spiritual or pure love can exist only by the unification of souls through body. Thus, physical love is a kind of way to attain the spiritual love. A Platonic lover is criticized by Donne because he cares only for the soul and not for the body. Excluding body and loving soul cannot provide us divinity because we are far away from satisfaction. One thing can be said about Platonic lovers that they find satisfaction only in loving souls but it cannot be applicable to all the lovers because we cannot separate body from the soul. If we try to separate the body from the soul, then we are not going to provide justice both to the body as well as the soul so how can we feel satisfied only by the soul not by the body. Metaphysical poets tried to show such kind of realities because we cannot deny that their concept of love is based on real experiences. A body cannot leave the soul before death and love is a kind of experience which provides us knowledge of both body as well as the soul. For poets like John Donne a Platonic lover cannot be a true lover because he is blind to see the reality. The sexual fusion of the body and the soul strengthens the divinity associated with love. John Donne has compared bodies with planets and soul with angels. Both of them that is to say the body and the soul are dependent on each other and thus they cannot exist without each other. If body is the vehicle then the soul becomes its driver and it is the responsibility of the soul to activate the body. The medieval concept of the ecstasy is different from the ecstasy of Donne. In the medieval period ecstasy was considered as a state of trance in which the soul is separated from the body and after separation it meets with the divine God. In Christianity, the term ecstasy means Holy Communion between the soul and the almighty. In John Donne, it is very interesting to find out that he has combined both philosophy and religion. The result of this combination is his concept of love. It is noteworthy to see that when he talks about body he moves very far away from the concepts of Platonic love. He advocates that lovers are brought together only through body. We can find that this poem is a kind of argument advocating ways of love and readers are about to judge this philosophy of love. It is only the readers who can understand and judge the concept of love associated with poets like John Donne. There is eroticism in the poems of Donne and Marvell mixed with divinity. There are references of bed, pillow which suggests the art of physical love associated with lover and the beloved. This sexuality is refereed by the poet as asexual because they are mating for the propagation of love. For this purpose the poet has used the image of a plant which reproduces asexually. Violets are blooming as it is the perfect time of spring in which they can bloom. The image of violet symbolizes faithful love between the lovers. The setting is pastoral which means that the love is natural. The detailed description of the poem will be a kind of bias to the metaphysical love but few lines from the poem is worthy to be quoted here-

> "Where, like a pillow on a bed
> A pregnant bank swell'd up to rest
> The violet's reclining head,
> Sat we too, one another's best.
> Our hands were firmly cemented."[7]

Close reading of the poem can make us understand the deeper meaning of the context. To some readers the metaphysical aspect of love is mystical in nature. According to Caroline Spurgeon

> "mysticism is, in truth, a temper rather than a doctrine, an atmosphere rather than a system of philosophy."[8]

This mysticism or atmosphere is related to all the poets who write on the subjects like love. While talking about the metaphysical concept of love it will be unfair if we exclude the poems of Andrew Marvell. *To His Coy Mistress* is a fantastic love poem. Here a nameless lover addresses his beloved who is also nameless. The lover stresses over a fact that he does not have much time to love. He is mortal and thus a subject to decay so he persuades his beloved that they should not waste the time and start loving each other. This poem is based on the theory of carpe Diem which means grab the day. Time is not going to spare any one. Either it is an insect or an animal, king or slaves, man or woman, everyone who is born is a subject to death. The lover has not much time left. He wants to love his beloved as the time of death is approaching. The lover warns the beloved that nobody can escape death as it is a universal truth. If she is going to refuse him then all the sexual desires will burn into ashes. Desires must be fulfilled and satisfied. There is nothing wrong in loving each other. Finally the lover presents an argument that nothing is going to change if they are going to love each other. The sun is not going to change its place and if they are going to love each other, then the time is also not going to stop but they can make the time pursue them. Some scholars have said that this lover is confused regarding sex. He tries to persuade his beloved by giving different logics and says-

> "…But at my back I always hear
> Time's winged chariot hurrying near;
> And yonder all before us lie
> Deserts of vast eternity.
> Thy beauty shall no more be found;
> Nor, in thy marble vault, shall sound
> My echoing song; then worms shall try
> That long-preserved virginity,…"[9]

Thus we can see that there is a thematic similarity between John Donne and Andrew Marvell. Both of them are best known for their philosophical love concepts. They are remembered as metaphysical poets. The form of love which Vidyapati talks about is different from these poets. Vidyapati is also a love poet and he has also written poems on sexuality. His ideas are platonic but he also talks about the beauty associated with the body. His poems are in fact more sensual then John Donne or Andrew Marvell. If we talk about love for spirituality then we can say that he is far ahead then Milton in terms of spirituality. His sensuality as well as spirituality proves that he was very far ahead of his contemporary poets. Future generations are blessed to have such a kind of inspirational source in form of a love poet. His poems have been translated in various different languages. The poems of Vidyapati are often quoted and they are the most amazing poems of sensuality. Few lines from the translated version of his songs can be useful quoting here-

> "Day by day her milk-breasts drew splendor.
> Wider her hips grew, her middle more slender,
> Love has enlarged her childlike gaze.
> Yea, all grace of childhood and childhood's ways
> Fall from their thrones and take sweet flight.
> Her breasts before were plums of light,
> Golden oranges next and then
> As bodiless love made bloom with pain…"[10]

The above quoted lines are taken from a love song and here Vidyapati has tried to throw some light over the love affair of a beloved. The physical beauty of the lady is far more expressive than any other poets. There are few scholars who have refereed Vidyapati as an obscene poet. If the poems of Vidyapati are obscene it means that we are biased for Platonic concept of love. There is nothing wrong in writing poems of love dedicated to a lover or a beloved. This kind of love is more realistic and expressive. These lines are melodious also and it can also be sung. In *The Wisdom of Poetry* Ezra Pound has tried to give a suitable definition of poetry. This definition is actually applicable to the functions of the poetry and is inspired by Dante where he says "melody which most doth draw...the soul into itself." [11]It means that after reading a true poem a reader is drowned into the words of the poet. This effect can be seen while reading the poems of all the sensual poets. Discussing the poems related only to man and woman love affairs will be unfair, as it is a very complex topic. The present chapter entitled Forms of Love encompasses all the explored and unexplored forms of love which exist in the society. It is a very tough but interesting task. We have seen the Platonic love, themes of Petrarchan sonnets and several other poems related to courtly love culture and among all those poems love remains at the centre. Apart from these love concepts we can also find poems dealing with love for the almighty. We cannot deny the existence of God but it is also right that nobody on this earth has seen God. It has been rightly said that God can be felt but it cannot be seen physically. In a normal love relationship it happens that when a lover loves his beloved, he watches her physically but if someone cannot see his beloved is it possible for him to love her? For loving someone, physical presence matters a lot but love for God can be an answer for this question. A devotee loves God more than his life but he is unable to see the almighty. His love is so real and so true that he presents himself to the almighty. Apart from this concept, we have also seen the concept of Platonic love. It says that the presence of body hardly matters. Soul must be unified for platonic love but nobody has seen soul yet there is love for the soul. Similarly, we have not seen God but we cannot deny the existence of God. John Milton has written *Paradise Lost* which is a kind of epic. It is said that Milton has tried to justify the action of God to the mankind. Milton loves writing spiritual poems. Love for God is not new and there are so many devotees who claim that they love God. Vidyapati has also written numerous poems addressing to the almighty. Love for God is also a form of love where we can see a very strong devotion. Poets like William Blake has said that Milton was supporting the devil's party then a question arises that if he was supporting the devil's party, then how can he love the almighty? Blake has expressed this opinion about Milton because in *Paradise Lost* the character of Satan is heroically written. Satan possessed several grand qualities which prove that he is the hero, which Milton has promoted. Shelley has also supported Blake and affirms that Satan is unmatchable in terms of heroic qualities. It is also correct that to oppose God the character of Satan must be strong. This can be one of the reasons that Milton has given heroic qualities to Satan. Actually Satan represents all the human beings who keep on fighting for their individuality and existence. Milton was a religious man and he followed the dictates of his religion minutely. He was a kind of person who tried to evaluate humanity in terms of religion. It is needless to doubt Milton's love for God. The devotional songs written by Vidyapati also prove that a true devotee can see God. There are some special eyes through which a devotee can see the almighty. His love for God is unique as it is a kind of trust which is impossible to break. Moving ahead of Spiritual love, we can find that among the poets of Elizabethan age William Shakespeare talks about male bonding. There can be a healthy relationship between a man and a woman but relationship between a man to the other man is very unusual. Shakespeare is in love with his friend and he says that in public, they should not accept that they are lovers, but in private they share a good time with each other. In public, the poet refuses each other's love because they are very much respected in the society. We can say that society plays a very crucial role in establishing a relationship between a lover and his beloved. We cannot deny that marriage is a kind of social contract which is signed by a husband as well as his wife. Love is a term which is very private in nature yet society acts as a check point to validate the love affair. This kind of validation or approval is directly linked with morality. It is also a fact that morality is not fixed and it is very tough to define it because it keeps on changing. For a lover, it has been considered as immoral to love a girl who is already married to some another person. It is also equally applicable to a lady and if she is married she cannot long for a lover other than her husband. Thus, society acts as a check point to manage a civilized colony. The term colony is negative as it hints to the practice of imperialism where we can find that a colony is treated like a slave. Thus, there is master slave relationship, but in a healthy relationship we cannot allow someone to be a master or someone to be a slave. We have already seen that during courtly love tradition there was a kind of master slave relationship between a lover and his beloved. The lover blindly followed his beloved as if the beloved was his guiding star. Such kind of love can be seen in the poems like *Astrophil and Stella* written by Philip Sidney. It is an English sonnet sequence which has one hundred and eight sonnets. The word Stella is Latin which means star and in the poem Astrophil is a star lover. The beloved is acting like a star and she is respected a lot by the lover. Scholars have also agreed to a fact that this poem is autobiographical in nature. Sidney is Astrophil himself whereas Stella is his beloved Penelope Devereux. Both Sidney and Penelope were betrothed when Penelope was a child. The marriage was broken because of some reasons, and later, she was married to another man whose name was Lord Rich. This marriage was also not a perfect marriage and Penelope lived a very unhappy life after her marriage. The poet discovers her marriage to Lord Rich in thirty first to thirty third sonnets. Astrophil is in a condition where he cannot cease his love for Stella. She is already married to some other person yet Astrophil is not ready to accept it. It is a very painful condition where a lover understands he has lost his beloved but he cannot live without her. The feeling can be understood in the songs and poems of Virah-Vedna written by Vidyapati, where the beloved says that she cannot live without her lover. It is a kind of pain coming out of the separation between a lover and his beloved. In vidyapati, we can find such emotions of Vipralambha Sringara in a very deeper way. Radha is feeling alone and impatient because she is not in a state to wait for her lover but here Astrophil cannot take it for granted that Stella has been married to some other man. Astrophil is going through a kind of agony and he still wishes that in any corner of her heart Stella could love him. Around the Sixtieth sonnet, Stella begins to generate some love and affection for Astrophil and it is at this point the lover starts feeling satisfied. The love story starts moving ahead and now the interaction between the two seems real. He is no more an admirer of her physical beauty but now his love for Stella is turning to be Platonic. The affair becomes very problematic for both the lover and the beloved because she is married to another man whom the society has approved. Stella is in a condition where she cannot accept the love of Astrophil physically, and thus, from both the sides the love becomes Platonic in nature. The bodies are not united but the two souls recognize each other as wife and husband and here, the society is also helpless. Love cannot be controlled by any institution, but it can be understood and felt only by a lover and his beloved. Astrophil feels satisfied with this kind of bonding but later his physical desire for her begins to grow. He fails in controlling his love for Stella and now he wants her physically. He feels restless and all the time he is busy thinking about her. There is a kind of conflict between his mind and the body. His mind thinks that he can please his beloved by suppressing his own physical needs but his body is unable to accept such doctrines. There are eleven songs in Astrophil and Stella and in the second song the lover kisses her while she is not responding because she is sleeping. This kind of kiss is not less then physical violence because she was ready for it. Stella feels very unhappy and annoyed because of this action of Astrophil, but the lover is still not ready to suppress his desire. This first kiss breaks the trust of Stella and she is prompted to reject him. It is admitted by her that she loves him but she also agrees that their meeting has become problematic so they should not see each other. The relationship becomes very complicated and both of them are separated. Even after the separation they feel love for each other. In sonnet number ninety three, the lover feels guilty and starts thinking that he has broken the trust of his beloved. This guilt gives us a hint that this lover is unhappy with himself and this love affair is going to end soon. Finally he is dismissed by Stella as a lover and Astrophil feels alienated yet he finds happiness in thinking that Stella is happy. In today's society, we seldom see such kind of relationship between a lover and a beloved. Such kind of relationship is rarely found and the poet has given feelings to his words and the readers are moved a lot after reading such a kind of beautiful poem. The poem *Loving in truth, and fain in verse* is a beautiful poem from the volume *Astrophil and Stella*. Few lines from the poem can suggest us the feelings of the lover-

" Loving in truth, and fain in verse my love to show,

That she, dear she, might take some pleasure of my pain,

Pleasure might cause her read, reading might make her know

Knowledge might pity win, and pity grace obtain,-

I sought fit words to paint the blackest face of woe;"[12]

The above lines clearly show the intelligence of the poet. He wants his beloved to obtain some grace. It is a very common thing for a beloved to extract pleasure from the pain of her lover. To love someone dearly is a painful act and the lover feels satisfied in that pain. Such kind of beautiful poetry is a kind of inspiration for all the love poets. Such a kind of lovely writing can also be seen in Vidyapati. In the poems of Virah–Vedna we have already seen the frustration of the beloved who is separated from her lover. It projects the intensity of love which can be felt only by a true lover. Apart from this separation of love we can also see another kind of love where a lover assumes that her beloved is virtually standing in front of him. Such kind of love can be seen in the poems of W.B.Yeats. Among his poems the most valuable to me is *Among School Children*. This poem was written when Yeats visited a convent school in Ireland in 1926. In the poem, the poet is moved to remember his early love, Maud Gonne. As the poet enters the school, he is received by a nun and he is taken into different classrooms. The children are amazed to look the poet who is now a Sixty year old man. When the poet looks at the children then he suddenly starts remembering Maud Gonne, his beloved. He thinks that Maud Gonne too would have been a student like these children. He remembers a particular day when she had complained him about the trivial incidents of school life. The poet had listened to her calmly and also expressed his sympathy to her. The poem becomes very special because places become very important when we are reminded about a happy past. This too happens with the poet who has gone to inspect the school but in spite of inspecting the school he is reminded about his beloved. His love for Maud Gonne is so deep rooted that he forgets his present role that he has come here to inspect the school. It proves that memory plays a very important role in our life as we may become happy or sad by remembering something associated with our past life. A girl is standing before the poet and the poet is visualizing Maud Gonne as a child. He is comparing the beauty and virtue of Maud Gonne with the girl who is standing before the poet. This sense of comparison can provide him satisfaction by thinking that in present life he is busy in thinking about his beloved. We are taken into surprise that suddenly the poet recalls Maud Gonne as an old lady. She is very old and weak, even her cheeks are hollow. It seems to the poet that the old Maud Gonne has become so old that he has forgotten his own age. Suddenly, he gains his consciousness and is reminded about the fact that he too is not a young man. He has also become older and weak. Once he was a very good looking guy but it is a fact that time and age spares none. Apart from all these forms of love, the most interesting and appealing love is love for nature. Romantic poets like Wordsworth, Shelley, Keats and Byron were all nature poets. They were free minded and they also wrote poems which directly appeals to our senses. Poems like *Tintern Abbey* are one of the most beautiful poems written by William Wordsworth. In this poem, Wordsworth says that once he had visited this place with his sister and now he has revisited this place. He is alone but remembers about the past. The poet writes –

"Of past existence- wilt thou then forget

That on the banks of this delightful stream

We stood together; and that I, so long

A worshipper of nature, hither came

Unwearied in that service: rather say

With warmer love- oh! With far deeper zeal

Of holier love. Nor wilt thou then forget,

That after many wanderings, many years

Of absence, these steep woods and lofty cliffs,

And this green pastoral landscape, were to me

More dear, both for themselves and for thy sake!"[13]

Wordsworth declares in the opening lines of this poem that this is his revisit to this place and he has revisited this place after five years. This place has become very special to him because memory of his sister is associated with this place. He mentions the object in his poem which he is seeing again but this time he is feeling lonely. Romantic poets like Keats and Shelley were also very inspirational and they have written very good poems. It is noteworthy to find that Shelley and Keats were not much recognized during their whole life span. They were highly criticized by the neo-classical critics. It has been pointed out that-

> "Shelley is depicting the fate of the romantic poet in the world of Eldon, Castlereagh and the quarterly review, as Milton that of the young Puritan poet in the world of laud and Strafford."[14]

This statement has been made about Shelley because his style of writing was bitter at several times. His concept of love was very unique and it is rarely found in modern poets. He was shocked in believing that the death of Keats was not natural and it was fastened by the comments in the Quarterly review on Endymion. Graham Hough said that-

> "Shelley ends with a Platonic or neoplatonic or Brahmanistic assertion that eternity alone is real, that the phenomenal world is an illusion, is Maya, a veil that hides us from the one true light."[15]

Shelley loved Keats so much that he was greatly moved by his death. He believed that after death, Keats became a part of universe and this kind of death can be seen as cosmic death. All these forms of love is a clear example of male bonding between two different poets. His poem *Adonais* is considered as a pastoral elegy which was written for John Keats in 1821. The opening lines of the poem says-

"I weep for Adonais- he is dead!

Oh, weep for Adonais! though our tears

Thaw not the frost which binds so dear a

Head!"[16]

Although we can see that Shelley mourns for the loss of such a beautiful poet but *Adonais* has some optimistic tones. It has been called as the most personal poem. In the poems of Vidyapati, we can also see the elements of male bonding which is very admirable. The poet loves Madhav as a person and feels inseparable with him. Scholars have argued that this kind of male bonding is not a true bonding because Madhav is God and the relationship established is between a devotee and his God. Love has many dimensions which has not been explored yet. It is the love which controls the worldly affairs. Even the cosmic affairs are controlled through some invisible force which is beyond our perception. We cannot give logics in the elements of love. Forms of love are numerous but all of them cannot be expressed because love is nothing but God itself.

NOTES AND REFERENCES

1. Abrams, M.H, *A Handbook of Literary Terms*, Wadsworth Cengage Learning, 2009,New Delhi. p 226

2. https://www.poetryfoundation.org/poems/45190/amoretti-lxxix men-call-you-fair

3. Prasad, B, *An Introduction To English Criticism*, Macmillan India Ltd, New Delhi, 2007.p 2

4. G.Wilson Knight, *The Wheel of Fire: Essays in Interpretation of Shakespeare's Sombre Tragedies*, 1930, Oxford University Press, London.p8

5. https://www.poetryfoundation.org/poems/46467/the-flea
6. Williams Oscar, *Master Poems of the English Language*, 1967, Washington Square Press, New York.p.370
7. Grierson, J.C, *Metaphysical Lyrics and Poems of the Seventeenth Century*, 1921,Clarendon Press, Oxford.p17
8. Spurgeon ,Caroline, *Mysticism in English Literature*, 1913, Cambridge University Press,Cambridge.p.2
9. https://www.poetryfoundation.org/poems/44688/to-his-coy-mistress
10. Aurobindo Sri, *Songs of Vidyapati*, Sri Aurobindo Ashram Publishers, Pondicherry,1956.p.5
11. Eliot,T.S, *Literary Essays of Ezra pound*, Faber & Faber Press, London,1954.p.25
12. https://www.poetryfoundation.org/.../astrophil-and-stella-1-loving-in-truth-and-fain-in...
13. https://www.theguardian.com/.../william-wordsworth-lines-composed-a-few-miles-abo.
14. Graham Hough, *The Romantic Poets*, B.I. Publications, New Delhi, 1980.p.146
15. Ibid.p.47
16. https://www.poemhunter.com › Poems › Adonais

****

Chapter Six

Fascination and Fantasy

In Literature, fascination and fantasy are two different things around which the plot and setting revolves. It is not only a play or drama but even the poetry section of Literature is affected by fascination and fantasy. Sometimes the readers are puzzled that fantasy can be treated as a genre and somebody can ask us about fantasy literature. It can be treated as a genre or a subgenre. We need to be sure that there can be different reasons for putting fantasy under any genre or sub genre. There are different genres like crime fiction, science fiction, horror fiction and many others. These fictions directly or indirectly are linked to fascination and fantasy. There can be different view points on this matter but the role of imagination in any form of fiction is very crucial. Genres can also be further categorized as genres of form or genres of subject matter. There should not be any confusion between these two types of genre. Crime fiction or detective stories are basically genres of form. This can be further exemplified as it has a recurrent style of narration, plot structure, dialogues and many more. It is interesting to see that even the characters used are archetypal in nature. This can be applied to fantasy or science fiction also. Ireneusz Opacki, who is a Polish genre critic have emphasized and discussed much more on this topic of genre and he talks about change in the types of genre which occurs in three ways-

> "The first is the creation of completely new elements of the language of poetry, in keeping with a completely new set of problems introduced by a given stage of history. Thus there arise new motifs, vocabulary, compositional devices. The second form is a semantic modification of the elements of poetics up to that time, as with a 'change in the meaning of an expression' in the evolution of language. In the history of the genre at this point two externally similar forms may appear – at different stages of its development; however they will be different forms, endowed with different meanings – like a pair of homonyms. And then it is impossible to combine them in a whole, in one variant or model of the genre; this is why the temporal boundaries of a specific genre model are so important. The third variety of evolution is the introduction within the field of one generic trend of elements belonging to specific, historically defined models of other genres."[1]

The above mentioned form of evolution of literary genres clearly presents an idea that at the end of the nineteenth century fantasy genre came into existence with a kind of certain modulations which will be discussed later. There are so many genres but all of them are not based on facts and realities. There are some genres which are based on data and collections. It is very interesting to see that there are several books which are based on imagination and fantasy. There are books dealing with children in which we can find several stories with pictures and in every picture there is some message. In fantasy literature, we can find different elements from different genres. In words of David Duff the key concepts of a genre are-

> "A term which, confusingly, is used in two almost opposite senses in modern genre theory: to denote the manner of representation or enunciation in a literary work (the three basic modes, in this sense, being the narrative, the dramatic and the lyrical – though the validity of this triad has been questioned); and to denote more strictly literary categories such as the tragic, the comic, or the pastoral, which are thematically specific but non-specific as to literary form or mode of representation. In this second sense, a mode is often distinguished from a genre, the latter term being reserved for types of literature which are both thematically and formally specific: tragedy as distinct from the tragic, comedy as distinct from the comic, etc."[2]

The terms used by Duff clearly gives us an insight that the three basic modes the narrative, dramatic and the lyrical which decides the form of literature. In fantasy and fascination, we can see that these terms are always associative in nature. Several scholars have treated fantasy as a mode which can mark its influence over genres like short story, poetry and the novel. This is also a fact that all the genres are interlinked and thus they are generic in nature. There are also several critics who have proposed that myth is a device through which fantasy can be propounded. This myth can be connected to romance as well. In the poems of Vidyapati there are certain myths which have been focused by the poet. These myths can have different branches like spirituality, divinity and love. Love can be divine and spiritual love can be mythical in nature but it is also right that every time it is not mythical as it can be real also. The role of fantasy is to provide a connecting link between mythical and real nature of the spiritual love. Myth and romance are far apart from each other, and thus, they both have their own existence. The definition of fantasy reveals that it is not real but unreal. Some impossible things are kept in the centre and the author or the poet tries to make plot upon this subject matter. Ireneusz Opacki, who is a Polish genre critic has discussed on the development of genres. We have already discussed his viewpoint but the romantic emphasis to create new subject which is unique brings forward a problem. The problem is large as in search of creativity the genres have changed a lot. Thus they are not formative but dynamic in nature. This change of dynamism can be understood by Duff's study of genre which says-

> "Another major development in genre theory which occurs in the romantic period is the recognition of the historical character of genres. To the modern reader this seems so obvious and fundamental a point that an effort of imagination is required to recall a time when it was believed that genres were static, universal categories whose character did not alter across time; and that it was therefore feasible to judge a work written in, say, 1750, by rules formulated in the fourth century, or to deny the existence of a new genre on the

grounds that Aristotle didn't define it. Yet such practices were absolutely orthodox before the advent of Romanticism, as almost any example of Neo classical criticism would illustrate. How they eventually came to be abandoned – in face of the irrefutable fact of the ascendancy of the novel, and the irresistible claims of an 'expressive' poetics – is a remarkable episode in the history of ideas. Its result was a new conception of genres as historically determined, dynamic entities, a view given fullest expression in Hegel's famous lectures on aesthetics."[3]

When we think about the ingredients of good poetry we have several questions in our mind including the genres. The problem lies in the fact that not a single answer can satisfy our mind. The modes of imagination lie in series in contemporary poetry. In modern and contemporary poetry, we cannot find the accurate theory dealing with Poetic imagination, although the romantic poets have shown their power of creativity and imagination in a great manner. Fascination and fantasy are the extended forms of imagination which we will discuss in detail in this chapter. Imagination is linked to different abstract forms like passion, feelings and emotion. It is actually a faculty of mind which successfully generates different kind of images associated with desires, aversions, passion and feelings. I have repeated feelings twice as it is the main constituent of imagination. It is very interesting to see that in similar situation different people have different imagination or set of images. The mental album varies from person to person. This is one of the basic reasons that every poet has his own imagination that is why there are different images used by different author. It also implies that in literature there can be the existence of different modes of imagination which can be kept together. Initially fascination was considered as memory but later the concept changes as memory is associated only with the past but fascination and imagination is timeless. In terms of time and place nobody can define imagination as it keeps on changing. Different forms of emotion are also not primary but secondary impression as it is not fixed but it also keeps on changing. According to David Hume "impressions"[4] are directed through senses as they are actually in form of ideas. There is a kind of interconnection between imagination and soul of the poet or the author. That is why; imagination comes directly from the soul of the poet although they are perceived through the sensory organs. The inter connection of imagination and soul was the concept behind the recognition of creative imagination. The soul of the poet is that area where superior work of art can be created through the tools of imagination. Thus, the working of imagination establishes a kind of dichotomy between the soul and the mind. This kind of dichotomy has a direct influence over the psyche of the poet as the imagination plays a subjective role in the psyche whereas the mind plays an objective role in the development of the psyche. This kind of poetic image which has been created by the soul of the poet has no cause but only effect. It is deep rooted in the consciousness of the poet which also inspires and motivates the readers who feel elevated after reading such a kind of masterpiece. Fancy is another term which has contributed a lot in the conceptualization of imagination. Initially it was thought that both these terms are synonyms to each other, but later it was found that both of them are not similar although they often come together. Some scholars have agreed that fancy embodies creativity in imagination. There is a kind of debate that fancy is inferior to imagination whereas imagination itself is superior to fancy as it has the power to create something new which is unique. During the Romantic period, imagination was connected to nature in poetry. It stresses over the power of imagination to recreate nature in terms of beauty. For poetic and creative power nature was considered very necessary during the Romantic period. This kind of co-existence between nature and imagination brings a kind of tranquility to the mind. It means that the poet's creativity is affected by the beauty of the nature which provides aesthetic pleasure to the poet. In other words we can also say that by the creativity of the poet, nature is recreated. Apart from this we should also understand the role of imagination in analyzing any work of literature especially poetry. Several men of letters agree that rational approach is needful in analyzing anything as analysis needs mind. It is a fact that without imagination we cannot approach to literature specially poetry because we need to understand the emotions recreated in words. Only rational approach cannot lead us towards the true analysis of poetry. When we read the poems of Vidyapati, we shall find that he has written on several topics including love. His spiritual poems cannot be understood only by the rational approach. His love poems are unique and special which needs sometime a lover's heart to understand. The role of imagination in poetry is like a tool whose job is to understand the reality. The definition of reality is also not easy, as it is a kind of admixture of real as well as unreal. Things which look unreal also exist in reality and when we understand it, then it happens that sometimes we cannot express it either verbally or in written. Here the role of imagination becomes very crucial and it helps the poet to extract reality out of the unreal. If a mother says that she does not love her child then we cannot say that she is telling the truth. It might happen that she really does not love her child but there is also a possibility that she is telling a lie because of some circumstances, as we all know that it is very hard to believe that a mother can say that she does not love her child. Similar situation can happen with spirituality. We all know that God exist but it is also a bitter truth that nobody on this earth has seen God. It is a kind of challenge to our belief system where we can believe only because we can feel God inside us. A devotee understands that whatever devotion song he sings in praise of God is not enough to make him see the physical presence of God. He can feel the God particle around or inside his heart but he cannot see God. Thus, the feeling of the almighty acts like an envelope in which the mind and the body of the devotee dwells. It is not an easy task to understand but it is also right that we cannot deny the existence of Krishna and Radha. We have heard a lot about Mirabai who loved God and for her everything was her God. This is a kind of belief system which can be extended further through our imagination. What we see is neither real nor unreal but it is a kind of admixture that is why it has already been mentioned that realism is an admixture of real and virtual. To understand this we need the wings of imagination whose task is creative not poetic. Imagination can be good or bad, it can be violent too. It depends upon the person and the situation. This is also correct that in modern times the horizon of imagination has changed. Earlier it was thought that poetic imagination was a part of human faculty. At that time the role of imagination was to create aesthetic artifacts. Through these aesthetic artifacts human experiences were shared. In modern times, this notion of imagination has been changed and now its role is to insulate and nurture the self interiority. It is further expressed through the use of images in poetry. The objective dimension of the picture or the image reflects the real life situation which turns to be objective in nature. It can be subjective also but it is very tough to create the subjective picture of real life experiences through words. To use an image as a picture of reality several things are to be kept in mind by an artist. In other words, we can say that these images have certain characteristics. Sometimes the image is specific and direct. When Shakespeare says that the lips of his beloved are not red it means that the lips were supposed to be red and beautiful. It was the notion that the lover should assign certain images to his beloved. During Elizabethan age the beloved was compared with the moon or she was like a shining star that the lover always followed. These images or pictures used at that time were real but when we read it today we understand that these images are exaggeration and the girl need not to be beautiful as moon. We also understand that moon cannot be so beautiful that it needs to be compared with the beloved. In modern times, the parameters have changed as there are so many scholars who think that moon looks ugly as it is dark and it has several marks which make it dull. Now it needs some explanation that as the age advances the parameters of comparison keeps on changing. It is also correct that an image is the representation of sensory perception. It is non decorative and exact, which means, it is the effect of what we perceive. In terms of poetic composition, it is the unit of the poem. It means that the poem emphasizes more on images rather than words. We can also say that too many abstract ideas reduce the firmness and concreteness of the images. In modern times, it has been the subject of examination by the

Imagists writers. There are different modes of imagination used during different situations of life as perceived by the authors. The non pictorial image reduces the role of imagination in poem. It is based upon facts and data and here abstractions are also used properly. It makes the prose composition good and noticeable. The idea behind this mode of writing is that certain poem needs to be measured as a good prose. This kind of technique reduces the use of creativity in writing poetry. It means that it is not necessary that every work of art is creative in nature especially poetry. Certain poems are written only to celebrate not to attain the height of creativity but firmness. It generally makes the poem dry and it is one of the reasons that this kind of writing is less in use now a days. The other mode of imagination which is used widely is pictorial imagination. It is a kind of imagination where things are imagined in its absence. Its absence does not mean that it does not exist but it means that it has an existence but from the occasion it is absent. It shows the creativity of the poet who deals with the object beautifully and draws the attention of the readers. Next kind of imagination is Fancy imagination in which sensory perceptions and memories are used to create new things. Here ideas are taken in the form of some mechanic association. By applying such a kind of association a predetermined pattern of art is unlocked by the author or the poet. Thus, we can also say that there is a kind of close affinity or association between fancy and imagination. In *Preface to Poems*, William Wordsworth has written about fancy and imagination. His understanding about fancy and imagination is not so simple to understand, yet it is so realistic in nature. It must be quoted here-

"Where there is more imagination than fancy in a poem, it is placed under the head of imagination, and vice versa"[4]

When the term fancy imagination comes together, it actually brings forward the notions of Romantic writers who used fancy as a mode of creativity. Fanciful creativity and creative imagination should not be understood as one, but both of them are two different things. Fancy was treated as a mechanical faculty by Coleridge. It needs talent to practice such a kind of art where we can find mechanical faculty. Poets like Fletcher, Ben Jonson and Pope are the masters of talent and their works are the lively examples of such a kind of imagination. Sometimes fancy was also associated with light hearted poetries whereas imagination was understood as a force behind serious form of writings. Romantic critics valued fanciful creativity less than imaginative creativity. They hardly cared for light hearted or intense poetry. Poetic imagination should not be confused with the idea of creation. Although both of them are closely attached yet there are several dissimilarities between them. Poetic imagination encompasses all the dimensions of creativity whereas imaginative creativity can stress more on the mechanical form of creativity. To understand this mechanical form of creativity, we need to understand the physicality of creativity. If we cannot see the ideas of creativity in concrete form than what is the benefit of imagination? It is a fact that nobody has seen imagination yet we believe that an idea or imagination can change the life of a person. The person might be a poet or any author or reader. in poets or writers the sensory mode of perceptions are very high that is why they are considered as the creators of fine poetry. It is very interesting to see that in modern age, myths and folklores are used in fantasy literature. It is applied to poetry also as it is the highest order of creativity. The modern poet, Shelley has called poets as the unacknowledged legislators of the world. We can find that in fantasy literature whether low or high, but myth occurs continuously. In love poems, this kind of imagination which includes myth can be seen frequently. It is one of the reasons that lovers are not rational in approach. We have discussed that reality is the admixture of real and unreal. Similarly, when we are talking about the role of myth in imagination and fascination, we need to understand that it is a kind of cultural instrument which converts the atmosphere as well as the surrounding into a coherent reality. Eric Gould in his famous book *Mythical Intentions in Modern Literature* has said that-

> "Myths apparently derive their universal significance from the way in which they try to reconstitute an original event or explain some fact about human nature and its worldly or cosmic context. But in doing so, they necessarily refer to some essential meaning which is absent until it appears as a function of interpretation. If there is one persistent belief in this study, it is that there can be no myth without an ontological gap between event and meaning. A myth intends to be an adequate symbolic representation by closing that gap, by aiming to be a tautology"[5]

Thus, we can see that Gould has beautifully conveyed the message that even surrounding and atmosphere understands the value of myth in expressing and analyzing the reality. To prove this point, we shall have to see the character sketch of the knight mentioned in Chaucer's *The Canterbury Tales*. Here the knight is supposed to be heroic in nature. It is a kind of myth, but even surroundings and atmosphere are ordered to express the truth. In reality, we can find that the Knight is chivalric in nature. In fact, he is one of the positive characters of Chaucer. Now some body can ask that why not the other characters have been justified by the poet? The knight represents the military group and in that period it was considered as the noblest profession after the church practices. Chaucer has tried to show us the reality of the time. In fact, he has done justice to almost all the characters and this is the reason behind his success. We can also see the character sketch of the Squire, who is the son of the Knight. He represents the secular pilgrims among the military group. They have the highest social status and are very famous in the society. Few lines are worthy to quote for this young man who was a lover also. There are some common symptoms present in every lover who is young as it is true that age cannot be a barrier to love someone.

> "With hym ther was his sone, a yong SQUIER,
> A lovyere and a lusty bacheler;
> With lokkes crulle, as they were leyd in presse.
> Of twenty yeer of age he was, I gesse.
> Of his stature he was of evene lengthe,
> And wonderly delyvere, and of greet strengthe.
> And he hadde been somtyme in chyvachie
> In Flaundres, in Artoys, and Pycardie,
> And born hym weel, as of so litel space,
> In hope to stonden in his lady grace.
> Embrouded was he, as it were a meede,
> Al ful of fresshe floures, whyte and reede;
> Syngynge he was, or floytynge, al the day,
> He was as fressh as is the monthe of May"[6]

He is described as a lover and a lusty bachelor. Here also, we can see that the myth is playing its role. The Squire was supposed to be a young man who is in love and was considered as a lusty bachelor. Here, the surrounding is supporting the reality of expression. He is fresh and young and like the church officials, he is not corrupt. Injustice has also not been done to the other characters because during the time of Chaucer, the condition of Church was really not good. Chaucer has only tried to show us the reality of that time. Now, we also cannot deny that it is also a myth that church officials were sinful in nature. It is ironical but mythical and things which are mythical in nature have the capacity to unfold the cultural development of the society. Moving ahead with this concept we cannot ignore the contribution of Samuel Taylor Coleridge who was considered as one of the greatest writers of his time. He is known as an English poet as well as a philosopher. He along with William Wordsworth is considered as the founder of Romantic Movement in England. *The Biographia Literiaria* is a discourse written by Coleridge is very famous and it is also interesting to see that it is autobiographical in nature. It was published in 1817 and we can find the detailed description of Fancy and Imagination in this book. It is a kind of literary theory or literary aesthetics. Here the elements of writing have been discussed. One thing is noticeable that although it is autobiographical in nature but it is loosely structured. There are several valuable judgments of the author in this book. Here he has also expressed his viewpoint on imagination. It is actually the work of a poetic mind on the external objects. We can say that through the wings of imagination, objects are treated as a subject and the subjects are treated as an object by the poets. This point will become clearer by an example. There is a Spanish ode entitled as *Ode to Tomatoes* written by Pablo Neruda. Here the poet has tried to write about nationalism through the objectified image of tomatoes. Few lines from the poem can make it clear and thus it is worthy to quote the lines-

> "The street
> filled with tomatoes,
> midday,
> summer,
> light is
> halved
> like
> a
> tomato,
> its juice
> runs
> through the streets.
> In December,"[7]

Neruda says that the streets are filled with common man and they are as common as tomatoes. Their blood is red like the juice of the tomato and in streets the blood flows. This poem is political but it has been written beautifully by the poet and the message is very clear. Thus here, the object in the form of tomato has been treated like a subject who is deep rooted in the mind of the readers. It is the role of imagination which can see the real in the unreal. The process of imagination needs to be understood properly. This process adds or subtracts some properties from the object which are visible to our eyes. Thus, from the object which we see something new is being created by our imaginative power. This imagination has been divided into two parts, by Coleridge, one part is primary whereas the part is secondary. Primary imagination acts like a primary agent which provides a kind of perception to almost all the human beings. In this kind of imagination, the outer world is perceived through our senses. It is universal in nature which is a kind of spontaneous act of the human mind. Secondary imagination is very special and it has also been referred as poetic vision. Here sensations act like a raw material and poetic creations are possible because of this secondary imagination. It is not easy to understand it quickly as it is special and it is not universal in nature. We can say that it is a kind of root of all the poetic creation. Coleridge has also given his views on fancy. It has been treated as inferior to imagination. Fancy is mechanical in nature whereas imagination is mysterious in nature. It is also right that imagination plays a very crucial role in writing poetry. A question arises in my mind that is there any rule regarding poetry's application on our imagination? Where to imagine or what should be the starting point of the imagination? For such questions, intelligence is required and scholars have agreed that no definite rules can be prescribed. Robin Skelton has remarked that-

> "Over-addiction to the exploration and exploitation of the purely subjective aspects of experience, obsession with non-intellectual, non logical processes of the subconscious is as mistaken as over-intellectualization or addiction to purely objective, mathematical, and definite ways of thought. The two must be combined, as in all good poems – certainly in the best of W.B Yeats, Dylan Thomas, Wordsworth and Blake- they invariably are."[8]

There are so many ideas regarding fascination and fantasy in literature. All these ideas are related to imagination. Several critics have agreed that they are the part of imagination. No doubt they are different branches of imagination but they are not similar in nature. There are few similarities as well as differences among them. We have already seen that even imagination have two parts one is primary imagination whereas the other is secondary imagination. Primary and secondary, they both are the parts of imagination, still they are not alike. Similarly, fascination and fantasy have certain variations. We have also seen that there is a separate genre of literature known as fantasy literature but this is also right that there is no separate branch for fascination. There is kind of coexistence between fantasy and fascination. If we will study more about fantasy literature we shall find that fascination is more interesting than fantasy. Normally we find that fantasy has a mystical base or we can say that it is mystic in nature. Sometimes it may be the supernatural elements or horror elements which are associated with fantasy literature. All these elements provide a dramatic nature to the poetry. A drama in poetry is created through the tools of fantasy and fascination. We cannot deny that there are dramatic elements even in love poetry, which is why; the readers are moved a lot by reading a good poem. According to Ronald Peacock-

> "… [Drama] can only emerge when the imagination functions in a quite special way, showing sympathy for all the innumerable and above all conflicting aspects of human character. For only then can it create the dramatis personae with interest and vividness, and lay the foundations for the dialectic of drama, in which

people react on each other, with all the situations arising in consequence. Whatever is said about life, philosophy, religion, morals, man or nature..."⁹

Such kind of functioning of imagination can be seen in the poems of Shakespeare, John Donne, W.B.Yeats and many others. In the poems of Vidyapati, we can see such elements rarely but it is noticeable. W.B.Yeats is famous for his exquisite form of writing but he is also fascinated to occultism. When he was a student in Dublin, he used to read articles related to occultism. It is interesting to see that it was not related to God but supernatural things. Several scholars have argued that his failure in love has made him more attached to occultism in the later phase of his life. He is very famous among the modernists as his use of symbols is unique. They appeal directly to the senses of the readers. His use of realism, romanticism and symbolism is a kind of allusiveness which is sometimes irrational but beautiful. He has contrasted the fantasy and the real in *The Circus Animals* and it symbolizes his creativity. In this poem, there are several images which are real as well as virtual. It seems that Yeats has given a new realm to the world of fantasy. Even in the poems of John Keats, we can see that the fusion of real and unreal has provided a new thought to his writings. He was a poet who is known to be romantic in nature. He took inspirations from the nature and he was also a very nice person. Romanticism in itself is a kind of escape from realism yet, Keats represented both. One of his poems *The Ode on a Grecian Urn* is a poem which expresses the inner conflict of the poet. This conflict is about love and pain. We can also say that it is a kind of conflict is between temporary and permanent. Life of human beings is temporary in fact everything which we see is a subject to decay. Nothing in this world is permanent and the poet is trapped between temporary and permanent, mortal and immortal. The image of the Urn is very dynamic. Its history, thoughts and emotions which provides it the colour of imagination is very attractive. It shows that beauty is truth and truth is the reality, which is a subject to decay. It is really beautiful as it encompasses the fantasy as well as the reality. In the poem *Ode To a Nightingale*, we can see that this poem is a kind of dream. The poet tries to escape from the real world. The imaginations are compact but fantastical in nature. One can experience the darkness of the night from the perspective of the nightingale surrounded by lofty trees. The realms of magic and fairies become alive here and we are taken into some another world. At the end of the poem, the imagination of the poet returns back to the real world. Such a kind of imagination is very fanciful for the poet. Coming back to the poems of John Donne, we have see that he has been referred as a metaphysical poet and his use of imagination is unbeatable. Helen Gardner has written about him that-

> "But his strong dramatic imagination of particular situations transforms the lyric and makes a metaphysical poem more than an epigram expanded by conceits."[10]

Metaphysical poets were known for their imagination and conceit. The kind of images which were used by the poets were very powerful and it was also farfetched. Such kind of imaginations was very fascinating. There are several poems written by John Donne in which he has used farfetched imagery and conceits. Those images are taken from the real world, but still, they are not real. I mean to say that even in the poems of Donne we can feel that real and the unreal both exist together. Thus, we can say that fascination and fantasy is a part of imagination and without imagination no great work of art is possible. For the poets like W.B.Yeats imagination was a very interesting subject. He even wrote poems on fascination and for him it was like a creative principle. For a modern reader, it is very important to justify the role of imagination in a poem or in a text. It also needs to be clarified that which kind of contemporary literature we are talking about? Is it about the literature of modern world which has so many genres, but very less rule for every genre? Such questions are very spontaneous in nature which is very figurative both in essence as well as tone. Contemporary literature has limited the role of fantasy, fascination or fancy in poems dealing with the subject like love and divinity associated with love. We can say that in contemporary literature a modern reader expects more from the poet as he is aware of the classical mode of writing poetry. In this matter, D.C.Allen has stated that it is very tough to read a poem according to the poet. We cannot understand the exact emotion of the poet in a single reading as it is very tough to understand the emotions hidden in words. He himself has said on this matter that-

> "I am convinced that it is impossible to read a poem as a contemporary of a poet might have read it. One can explain lost references, one can annotate the poem from the historical remnants of its generation, but this is not giving it a contemporary reading. If we are told 'let us read this poem as a contemporary' we might ask which contemporary the reader has in mind. Since I cannot come close to reading an Elizabethan as an

Elizabethan could, I can hardly have the bad taste to argue that I know how Spenser, Shakespeare or Marvell wrote a poem."[11]

Finally, it is also correct that the effect of a poem is all about reader's response. It is always an easy task to make simple generalizations of any work of art but it is not trustworthy. Several critics have different points in their mind and analysis depends upon the time and the subject matter of the poem written by the poet. I have mentioned time because it is associated with era. In different time and perspective, different ideologies keep on changing. The concept of love remains the same but expression has changed. In modern times, writing poems for a beloved and following her blindly is not an easy task. The role of imagination has also changed. Fascination and fantasy have also gone under a phase of metamorphosis. Apart from this, the thing which is the matter of our concern is the capacity of a thought or imagination to make an appeal to our senses. This concept has not changed. Time and age will keep on moving but this concept is the prime concept and it is not going to change. In every age, the authors have tried to focus on their subject matter which will attract the readers. This attraction can happen only if the literature appeals to the senses of the readers. The recreation of feelings into thought or the changing of thought into a perfect feeling can be the right kind of subject matter for a mature poet. T.S.Eliot has commented on this-

> "When a poet's mind is perfectly equipped for its work, it is constantly amalgamating disparate experience, the ordinary man's experience is chaotic, irregular, fragmentary. The latter falls in love or reads

Spinoza, and these two experiences have nothing to do with each other, or with the noise of the typewriter or the smell of cooking, in the mind of the poet these experiences are always forming new wholes."[12]

The essays written by Eliot entitled *The Metaphysical poets* and *Andrew Marvell* appeared in 1920. These two essays were written to define the metaphysical aspects of poetry as well as the Caroline imaginations of writing poetry. It is also a kind of criticism of John Donne. In these two essays, there are some seminal ideas which were taken warmly by so many scholars and critics. F.R.Leavis has written about Eliot that-

"The irresistible argument was, of course, Mr. Eliot's creative achievements, it gave his few critical asides – potent, it is true, by context- their finality and made it unnecessary to elaborate a case."[13]

These quotations are very relevant to understand this chapter. Fascination and fantasy is like a tool which is handled with care by the poets like John Donne. He has written several poems and in fact those ideas have been referred as metaphysical in nature. It is very important to understand that Metaphysical is nothing, but association of different forms of fascination and ideas with the existing ideas in form of reality, which we cannot understand in a concrete form. In the poems of Vidyapati, these elements are also present and we will be surprised to see that during that period of time how can a poet think much ahead of his time. There are several things which are common in Vidyapati and John Donne, but we cannot discuss those elements in this chapter as there is a separate chapter to study the similarities and dissimilarities between these two poets who are the legends of their own time. It is interesting to see that F.O.Matthiessen views Donne similar to Eliot and says that-

> "The jagged brokenness of Donne's thought has struck a responsive note in our age, for we have seen a reflection of our own problem in the manner in which his passionate mind, unable to find any final truth in which it could rest, became fascinated with the process of thought itself. What he strove to devise was a medium of expression that would correspond to the felt intricacy of his existence, that would suggest by sudden contrast, by harsh dissonances as well as by harmonies, the actual sensation of life as he himself had experienced it. His great achievement lay in his ability to convey his genuine whole of tangled feelings." [14]

This tangled feeling is not an easy task to express on paper. In my opinion, every great poet or author can find themselves in similar situations. Fascination and fantasy are the tools which needs extra care to be handled properly. Right use of words on right situation has always been a bone of contention for poets and authors. Vidyapati, as I have mentioned earlier that he is a kind of poet who is very sensible in choosing words for a proper feeling. His fascination is not entangled as he is able to find the final truth with the help of his imagination. In spite of all these details, there is the Romantic Imagination which seems to me as an extended version of Vidyapati. Although there is very little connection between Vidyapati and Romantic poets but still in modern literature it can be a helpful comparison. Above also, I have tried to configure some connections between these two different sects of poetry but now some point needs to be understood clearly. If I wish to compare one characteristic feature which differentiates the British Romantics from Vidyapati of fourteenth century, it must be found in the importance which was given to fantasy and imagination prevailed during that period. On this view, we can figure several significant differences on every points of minute description. In Fourteenth as well as Eighteenth century, we can see that in poetical theory imagination was not considered as a cardinal point. For critics like Johnson and Pope and much before Dryden, it has some importance which was limited in nature. Fancy was approved as a vehicle of Judgment. The apt use of symbols and images were also admired. For these above mentioned critics and writers, what was the most valuable thing in poetry was the use of truth in emotions. They always wished to express themselves in general terms so that people can have trust on them. Poetry does not mean a massive lump of complex ideas but it needs to be understood by common men. Imagination was a kind of belief and for a Romantic writer imagination is fundamental and it was considered by all the Romantic writers that it was not possible to write poetry without imagination. This belief system was a kind of contemporary belief for the poets. They were conscious enough that they were capable to create an imaginary world of their own which can be very beautiful. This imagination was further strengthened by several considerations which were metaphysical and religious. It was equally true to Vidyapati also, who was very optimistic for making his own imaginary world where he can devote his time to worship. To him, love was also a kind of worship and we have seen several examples for it. Coming back to the Romantics we can see that John Locke has dominated English Philosophy with his special theories. It was assumed by him that a human mind is passive in perception. It was well suited because it was under scientific speculation and it has some roots to Newton. Both Newton and Locke found that God exists in the universe. John Locke supported the existence of God on the behalf that-"the works of nature in every part of them sufficiently evidence a deity"[15] whereas Newton has certain mechanics in mind and he also accepted that God was present to handle the mechanics of the world. It was not religious but it was a kind of question which has more feeling and less reasoning. It was a matter of experience not argument. It was also true to the poetry of all kind. John Locke considered poetry as wit and it was thought that the job of wit was to accumulate, ideas so that, it can have a pictorial and idealistic representation of life and "thereby to make up pleasant pictures and agreeable visions in the fancy"[16]. He also considered wit as irresponsible which has no connection with truth or reality. The poets of Romanticism have rejected this theory and they have established the connection of imagination in poetry. Such kind of poetry is unique in nature as it was always inspired from nature. In the words of William Blake –

> "This world of imagination is the world of Eternity; it is the divine bosom into which we shall all go after the death of the vegetated body. This world of imagination is infinite and Eternal, whereas the world of Generation, or vegetation, is Finite and Temporal. There Exist in that Eternal World the Permanent Realities of Every Thing which we see reflected in this Vegetable Glass of Nature. All Things are comprehended in their Eternal Forms in the divine

body of the Saviour, the True Vine of Eternity, The Human Imagination." [17]

For Blake imagination is like God as it gets operated in the soul which is immortal. Any creation is divine if it has been created by imagination because here the spiritual nature of any human being comes out and creates the divinity. For Vidyapati we have already seen that his sense of imagination is very trustworthy as he is a kind of poet who needs to be celebrated. His imagination is divine in itself as spirituality is marked in each and every sentence of his devotional songs.

NOTES AND REFERENCES

1. Opacki, Ireneusz. *'Royal Genres.'* *Modern Genre Theory*. Ed. David Duff. Harlow: Longman, United Kingdom, 2000. P.119.

2. Duff, David. *Modern Genre Theory*. Harlow: Longman, United Kingdom, 2000. P.47

3. Ibid.p.4

4. Hume, David. *A Treatise of Human Nature*. Edited by L. S. Selby-Bigge, 2nd ed. Revised by P.H. Nidditch. oxford: Clarendon Press, Oxford, 1978. P.75

5. https://books.google.co.in/books?isbn=1400886252

6. Gould, Eric. *Mythical Intentions in Modern Literature*. Princeton, N. J.: Princeton University Press, 1981.p. 6

7. https://poemanalysis.com/ode-to-tomatoes-by-pablo-neruda-poem-analysis/

8. *The Poetic Pattern* P.88
9. The Art of Drama London 1960, second impression with some corrections, p.178
10. Introduction to *The Metaphysical Poets*, London, 1959, pp 22-23
11. Baltimore, *Introduction to Image and Meaning Metaphoric Traditions in Renaissance Poetry*, 1960.p.7
12. *The Metaphysical Poets* p.273, it is also found in other critics like F.R.Leavis, in Imagery and Movement, *Scrutiny*, vol xiii
13. *Milton's Verse, Scrutiny*, vol ii, September 1933, p.123
14. Williamson G, The Donne Tradition, Massachusetts,1930,pp48
15. These lines have been taken from *The Reasonableness of Christianity* written by John Locke, 12th edition.
16. Cited from *An Essay Concerning Human Understanding* by John Locke.
17. Blake, William, *A Vision of the last Judgment*, The Nonesuch Press, London 1939, p.639.

****

Chapter Seven

Conclusion

Vidyapati was a Poet of Rasa which is considered as the final goal of any kind of literature. He has written several poems which are famous in almost all the corners of India. At a time there were several critics who were busy in finding the linguistic peculiarities of Vidyapati. Some considered him as a poet of Maithili literature whereas some treated him as a Bengali poet. Thus we can see that he was claimed as a poet of different languages. It is his versatile nature that he understood the literary taste of that time. He was a contemporary of poets like Chaucer and Langland. Like Chaucer he has also done several modifications in Maithili literature .So many new words were used and discovered by him. We can say that he has experimented with almost all the genres of poetry. Rasa is considered as soul of poetry as it is only through Rasa a particular emotion or sentiment can be created. Vidyapati is a kind of poet who has written extensively about different kind of Rasas. There are Questions or doubts on which different scholars and critics agree that Vidyapati is a devotional poet whereas there are also several facts which discloses that he was the poet of Rasa. How can a devotional poet write the poems of Rasa? Was he a devotee or follower of Rasa theory? The answer becomes very easy with a fact that he was a devotee of the almighty, who has gifted him so many talents all together. He wrote both devotional songs as well as love poems and all of his creations are celebrated. His poems were written in fourteenth century but it is applicable to all the times. Today also these poems are read and sung and it seems that Vidyapati is alive in our heart. It is the gift of art that his poems and other writings have made him immortal. Vidyapati has written about all the kinds of human feelings and emotions in his poems. We can also say that we can find all the eight forms of Rasa in his poems and songs. He has emphasized more on the topics like love. His song of Radha and Krishna encompasses all the horizons of love or relationship between a man and his beloved. He believes in every aspect of sringara and writes about sambhog, that is, union between a lover and his beloved as well as vipralambh which is the anguish of love because of separation. It is also known as virah-vedna. Even Kalidasa has written about this form of love in *Meghdutam* . The poems of Vidyapati have added new dimensions in the whole canon of Indian Literature especially in poetry. In the poems of *Deh-chhavi* so many expressions have been written about the youthful life of Radha. Her beauty has been praised by the poet and it seems that Radha is the most beautiful lady of the world. Her beauty has been explored so well that it invokes the initial stages of Sringara Rasa. One of the prime and noticeable things in Vidyapati is his selection of language. He has selected Maithili language in the age when Sanskrit was at its highest prominence. The religious doctrines were also not in favour as there were continuous ups and downs in the religious belief of the people. The rise of Islam was another factor which was considered as a threat to the empire of Mithila. During that time, Vidyapati selected Maithili as his major language of expression through the use of his poetry. It was a very brave step which was certainly praiseworthy. In *Astadhyayi* which is a grammar book by Panini we can find several technical terms. Panini has accepted that an author must write in a language in which he feels comfortable. It must be taken into notice that the words and sentences used by Vidyapati in his poems are very comprehensive and it embraces almost all the corpuses of Maithili language. As a poet Vidyapati always aimed to portray the eternal beauty of mankind. The superficial study of Vidyapati can misguide us to a particular thinking that he wrote about eroticism. There are several critics and scholars who have said that there are erotic elements in the writings of Vidyapati. The poet has written about human beauty and he has tried to explore the internal as well as external form of beauty and there is nothing wrong in it. We must analyze his poems from all the angles and the charge of eroticism can be justified only if we are prejudiced with several misleading notions about the poet. By reading his devotional songs, love poems and other poems dedicated to nature we can find our heart and soul satisfied as the poems gratifies and touches all the dimensions of human affairs. Mahakavi Kalidasa has written about the beauty of Shakuntala as she is a form of divinity. God has created her with charm and tenderness. Vidyapati has taken this form of beauty and he has done some modifications in the concept of beauty. He writes about the beauty of Radha that she has been created by the rays of moon and her brightness reflects the brightness of the almighty. Wherever she goes, she modifies the surroundings and an aura of divinity and beauty is created. It shows that Vidyapati is a natural genius. Addison has tried to differentiate between the artful genius and natural genius. He writes that-

> "Natural genius is like a rich soil in a happy climate, that produces a whole wilderness of noble plants rising in a thousand beautiful landskips, without any certain order and regularity. In the other it is the same rich soil under the same happy climate, that has been laid out in walks and parterres, and cut into shape and beauty by the skills of the gardener."[1]

After finding the concept of Addison, we are bound to think that whether a poet is made or born? The answer of this has been given by Aristotle when he says that-

> "Poetry demands a man with a special gift for it, or else one with a touch of madness in him."[2]

It is doubtless that Vidyapati was a born genius who was embedded with several special qualities, and, we can find both the modern as well as classic elements in his writings. T.S.Eliot has identified two features of a classic: the maturity of idioms and the maturity of manners. Virgil in his *Aeneid* also acts like a justification for Eliot and we can also say that it is only in Virgil's *Aeneid* we can find the enactment of Eliot's definition. Frank Kermode has said that this definition of Eliot is too imperialistic and thus he has tried to give a more liberal view. According to him, a classic poet or writer must have patience and it must not change with time. It is further endured that classics are expected to act according to time and space and it also depends upon the culture and tradition that what are the real expectations from a classic. It has been proved that time and space cannot spoil the infinite beauty of a classic. In all the definitions of the classic, we can find that Vidyapati acts like a role model for any classical form of poetry. Among the vaishnav sects of Bengal, the poet Vidyapati was very popular because of his devotional songs and love poems. He was given a title of Kavishekhar[3] by the vaishnav devotees of Bengal and it was like a pride of honour for him . There is a fusion of lyricism and sweetness in his poems. In Devi-Vandana[4], the poet Vidyapati has written about shakti associated with Matri. Here Matri can be understood as deity which is always feminine but powerful. Wife of Shiva has created fear among the devils and she is capable to change the atmosphere of any place. He seeks solace from her. The song is entitled as Bhairvi song and still today it can be heard anywhere in the region of Mithila and nearby areas. The song is so popular that even a child is capable to recite the full song with dignity. In the next song of Devi-Vandana, Vidyapati remembers all the nine forms of Goddess Durga who is associated with Shakti. In the poem of Janaki-Vandana[5], Vidyapati has tried to please Goddess Sita. In her, we can find a proper code of conduct expected from a daughter or a wife. There are several criticism regarding the code of conduct expected from a woman in a typical Indian society. We are not supposed to explore such extensive form of criticism. In the poems dedicated to Shakti cult, we can see that the fierce form of a deity has been portrayed so that the devils fear from the deity. The feminine form is associated with beauty and when it comes to the fearful form of Shakti, we find that the aggressive form of a female has been shown which is very dangerous. There are a lot of forms given to the divinity especially in Hindu religion. Shiva is also known for destruction and all the devils are scared of Lord Shiva because he is capable to punish them for their faults. It should be taken into account that the fierce form associated with the divinity has been shown in other religions also. Even in several English Poems, we can find such references. In one of the poems of T.S.Eliot entitled *Gerontion* , there are few lines which needs to be quoted here-

> "Signs are taken for wonders...
> The word within a word, unable to speak a word,
> Swaddled with darkness. In the juvescence of the year
> Came Christ the tiger."[6]

Here Jesus Christ has been portrayed as an infant and in contrast to the image of a infant who cannot speak anything, the angry and terror full aspect of divinity associated with Christ has been invoked here. This terrorizing image is a kind of anti thesis for the weak and gentle lamb which is again a form of God. It can be understood by other poem *The Tyger* written by William Blake. A few lines from the poem can make us understand that softness and kindness is a form of God but frightening image is also a form of God whose projection is very much essential so that the weak and submissive creatures of God must be safeguarded. William Blake writes-

> "Tyger Tyger, burning bright,
> In the forests of the night;
> What immortal hand or eye,
> Could frame thy fearful symmetry?"[7]

Thus, it becomes clear that the lamb as well as the tiger is a form of Christ. When there is a need to show the wrath of God then the image of the tiger is automatically projected. So in any religion the form of the almighty can change but the function remains the same, that is, to maintain a proper balance in nature in form of justice, mercy and wrath. In the poems of Vidyapati, devils fear Goddess Durga as she represents Shakti. In Christianity, the tiger is also a form of Jesus Christ and we have just now seen it. The Shakti cult of Vidyapati or in the poems of T.S.Eliot and William Blake, it is now proved that unfair means are a subject of punishment and the almighty has his own ways and forms to punish the devils. The feminine form of the almighty is represented through various deities like Durga and Kali. At the same time, in Sita we can find the feminine form of the almighty in terms of beauty and duty. Either it is Jesus Christ or Goddess Durga, both are fearful but only for the devils. For devotees both of them have a proper place of worship. Our topic is love traditions and it needs to be noticed that a Satan or a devil wants to be punished by the hands of God because they love God. They want a mortal blow from the God so that they will remain immortal. They will be remembered by the devotees that once they were killed by the hands of the almighty. It is the greatness of Vidyapati that he has also written his poem on river Ganga. By reading his Ganga-Stuti, we are surprised to find the dedication of the poet. He considers river Ganga as mother Ganga who nurtures the nearby areas and the people living on the banks of river Ganga also treats her as a deity. It is the greatness of Indian tradition that river Ganga has a sacred place in the whole Indian mythology. When Vidyapati leaves the bank of Ganga he feels that he is crying because he is going away from his mother. She is the symbol of purity and in Indian mythology, it is considered that all the sinful activities are washed away by her touch. It is sweet and serene and the poet find solace at the bank of river Ganga. He expects that circumstances may bring him near mother Ganga time and again so that he can share the moments of happiness and despair of his life with mother Ganga. Vidyapati is so sensitive regarding the purity of mother Ganga that he thinks that he has committed some mistake because he has touched her with his feet. He also requests to mother Ganga that he wants to remain with her even at his time of death. This is the reality of Indian mythology that we consider Ganga not as river but as a mother. There are so many poems written for river Ganga but Vidyapati acts like a leader to all those poets who have written poems on this subject. Dead bodies are often brought near the bank of Ganga as it is thought that the soul of the dead person rests in peace if the body gets a glimpse of river Ganga. It is considered that Ganga is the daughter of Brahma who has the ability to destroy all the sins of the sinners and she is so kind that in return she wants nothing. She also touches the head of Lord Shiva and keeps him calm. This is one of the reasons that she is worshipped even by Gods and deities. T.S.Eliot has also mentioned about river Ganga in his poem *The Wasteland* and he writes-

" Ganga was sunken, and the limp leaves
Waited for rain, while the black clouds
Gathered far distant, over Himavant."[8]

Eliot also understands the greatness of river Ganga. People know that the water of Ganga is capable to purify their body and soul so that they can escape the cycle of life and death. Eliot imagines that with the increase of sinners in the world River Ganga was sunken by God. Himavant[9] is a reference to the peak of Himalayas. T.S. Eliot wanted a change that may the wrath of God fall on all the sinners so that the world itself will be purified because everywhere there is a wasteland which needs to be improved. One can produce his argument that in Indian mythology river Ganga has a very special place and if somebody is going to write on such subjects then automatically his writings will be celebrated. This is not the exact situation with Vidyapati. There are so many poems which have hardly any connection with Indian mythology yet the poems are very famous among the readers. It is also a kind of misconception that only in India rivers are considered as sacred and pure. Rivers are treated as mothers and they are very sacred worldwide. India may be a leading country in giving respect to the nature's bounty but wherever human population is there we can find respect for rivers, mountains and all the objects of nature which ensures life. Generations after generation have witnessed the greatness of nature's bounty. George Gordon Byron has written in *Chile Harold's Pilgrimage* that-

> "There is a pleasure in the pathless woods,
> There is a rapture on the lonely shore,
> There is society where none intrudes,
> By the deep sea, and music in its roar:
> I love not Man the less, but Nature more,
> From these our interviews, in which I steal
> From all I may be, or have been before,
> To mingle with the universe, and feel
> What I can ne'er express, yet cannot all conceal."[10]

In first canto of the poem we can find that the beginning is done by a kind of invocation and later the character of Childe Harold is explored. He is searching for better qualities of manhood to which Vidyapati's *Purusparikcha* can be an answer. He gets haunted by the evil deeds. Byron finds pleasure in the pathless woods which is lonely. The rapture on the lonely shore clearly reveals that the poet is enjoying his seclusion whereas it is considered as a precursor of sorrowful feeling. The poet is enjoying nature and it does not mean that he is feeling secluded with the moods of sadness. In poems of Vidyapati, we can also find that first of all he invokes the almighty and he is a kind of poet who is in love with nature. In his poems, we can find the full description of natural objects. Rivers are also a part of nature and it is a well known fact that water supports life so only a mother can give life to a child. This can be the reasons that Vidyapati calls river Ganga as mother Ganga. If we read the opening lines of the poem *Kubla Khan* written by Coleridge, we can find that there is river Alph which is considered as sacred by the poet. The poem begins with-

"in Xanadu did kubla khan

A stately pleasure-dome decree:

Where Alph, the sacred river, ran

Through caverns measureless to man

Down to a sunless sea."[11]

The poem describes Xanadu which is a place of Mongol emperor. The poet then tells about a river which makes the nearby area fertile. There are not much comparisons between Coleridge and Vidyapati but we will find that in terms of imagination Vidyapati exceeds Coleridge. In the poems of

Shiv-Vandana[12] Vidyapati has opened his heart so much as a devotee that we feel surprised. His songs of devotions are amazing as he has admired the form of Lord Shiva in a very splendid way. He has talked about Shiva that he is known as Ardhnarishwar[13] and for devotees pleasing God has always been a very tough task. Songs of Vidyapati are also sung today so that Lord Shiva may come in front of the devotees. The poet has also written poems which suggest that there is uniformity in the presence of Vishnu and Shiva. Thus the poet has tried to bring unity in Shaivite and Vaishnavite communities. These features of the poet can be seen in Greek Poetry where poets admire God like human beings. Homer has written *Iliad* and in the poem he has described several physical features of God. The story of the poem covers the Trojan War and in that war there is participation of God also. The hero of the war is Achilles. There is a story related to Achilles that he was considered invulnerable who could not be defeated. Only his heels were weak and the only way to kill him was to strike over his heels. When he was born he was dipped into river Styx by his mother Thetis and by doing so, all the body parts of Achilles was dipped into the river except his heels. Thus, his heels became weak but still he was a Trojan hero who could not be defeated in any war. It was all possible because of the magical river Styx. There is no need to write about the Trojan War hero Achilles here but I can find out some similarities between Achilles and Bhisma, the eighth son of Kuru king Shantanu. Achilles and Bhisma both are the warriors and it was impossible to defeat them in war. Achilles was the son of Peleus and Nereid Thetis. The father of Achilles was mortal whereas the mother was immortal because she herself was a goddess. Bhisma is also known as Gangaputra because his mother is Ganga and we have seen earlier that Vidyapati has written poem on river Ganga. She is the symbol of purity and also a sacred river. She is also a goddess who is immortal. Generations after generations will come and die but Ganga shall remain firm, pure and serene. Thus the Trojan war hero Achilles and Bhisma of Mahabharta both of them have certain similarities. We can see certain parallels between the devotional songs of Vidyapati and the Poets of Greek Literature. In both the literature, poets are very serious regarding description of their Gods. In Krisna-Vandana[14], Vidyapati has described the beauty of lord Krishna. He has compared the beauty of Krishna with several objects like moon and different precious stones. He says that Sri Krishna has eternal beauty which cannot be matched with anything. Thus we find here that Vidyapati has compared the beauty of Krishna with objects like moon and precious stones but he has agreed that no form of beauty can stand in front of Krishna. Thus his beauty is matchless and ageless. Scholars and critics have said that beauty is associated with females, and thus, it is a kind of virtue associated with Radha but Krishna is also beautiful and it means that in every individual both masculine and feminine quality is present in parts. Beauty of Sri Krishna is a reality which is mixed with pride and valour. In Indian tradition Lord Sri Krishna holds a very special position among Gods. There are numerous examples in Indian mythology which shows that from his childhood Sri Krishna was a magician who was able to take any shape and form. He was loved by almost all the men and Gods. Vidyapati praises him as he wants his blessings. The poet writes that a man keeps himself very busy in worldly affairs and thus he forgets God. He finds himself lost in maintaining relationships in form of a friend, son, and brother, and thus, there is hardly any time left for the worship of God. At the time of death a man realizes that he was too busy to remember the almighty. In despair he looks here and there and thus he repents. The almighty is so kind that he expects nothing from the human beings. Vidyapati tries to invoke God as he knows that without God's grace he cannot do anything. He needs the continuous blessings of God. After the devotional poems Vidyapati has written poems on youthful life. In the life of a girl there are so many changes when she enters in the youthful life. Her physical as well as the mental features changes a lot. First of all, she feels a lot of problem as she is unable to understand the changes within her. Childhood has just gone and she has entered into a new life. Her eyes have started playing with the advancement of age and maturity. Her way of speaking has also changed and it seems that there is no more children like appearance left in her. She looks very beautiful and her beauty is like the beauty of the moon. When she takes the vanity box in her hand she looks herself in the mirror and asks with her friend about the elements of love. She wants to know about the stages of love as it seems that she has been haunted by some desires. In seclusion, she watches her breasts and laughs because once they were very small and now they have become bigger in shape. Vidyapati says that she has a perfect feminine beauty and charm. She is beautiful enough to create sensations in the heart of her lover. It seems to the poet that at the beginning there is a continuous struggle between childhood and adulthood and both of them are trying to defeat each other. We can also say that there is a continuous struggle between the realms of innocence and experience. Now, the days of childhood have gone so in the struggle between the world of innocence and experience there is no chance for innocence to come back. It is a proven fact that time and tide waits for none. Time has arrived when the maiden can feel sexual desire in her heart. She asks her friend about the sexual act of love. Vidyapati has compared the physical beauty of a woman with the statue of lord Shiva. The sexuality associated with a woman tends to produce Sringara Rasa whereas the statue of Lord Shiva acts as a central point of devotion. The poet has mixed sexuality with spirituality and thus we are reminded about John Donne who too combines sexuality with spirituality in his poems. It has proved earlier also that Metaphysical poets thought that the spirituality can be gained through the sexual act. Soul is within the body and it can be separated from the body at the time of death. When a lover performs the act of love with his beloved than the soul of the lover as well as the beloved come out and unite. This unity is not less than attaining divinity. Thus Vidyapati and Metaphysical poets share a common view point here. Metaphysical poets came very late so we can also say that there is a chance that the idea of Vidyapati must have been copied. It can be possible or it cannot be possible but we cannot deny that Vidyapati was a born genius who was very ahead of his own age. Maithili Literature has been enriched by the jewels like Vidyapati. In the poems of Vidyapati we can find invocation to God, deities as well as nature. In the opening poem *Alastor* , Shelley also produces a sense of invocation not similar to Vidyapati but it needs to be mentioned here that-

"Serenly now

And moveless, as a long- forgotten lyre...

I wait thy breath, Great parent, that my strain

May modulate with murmurs of the air...."[15]

In *Adonais* Shelley has used expressive words for natural objects like wind. The poem is written in a classic way which parallels the earlier poems of Romantic age written on the theme of dejection. This theme of dejection is missing in

Vidyapati but in terms of natural beauty there are some common elements between Shelley and Vidyapati. We can find archaic words in both these poets. Although Shelley is a Romantic poet but his use of symbols and images are not common to the other Romantic poets. In the poems of Pranay-Prasang[16], Vidyapati uses extensively the symbols and images related to love. Krishna and Radha both are in love with each other. They feel satisfied at the glance of each other. The most important and valuable aspect of love lies in Vipralambha Sringara. This can be defined as a kind of love in separation. It is a more frequent Rasa which can be seen in the poems of Vidyapati. In Kalidasa's *Abhijnanasakuntalam*, we can find this form of love genuinely expressed. The union of Shakuntala and Dushyanta is very brief and in most of the time Dushyanta feels that he has been entrapped in a love-sick condition. It is heightened when Dushyanta finds all of his memories associated with the ring. Suddenly he remembers Shakuntala with his full heart. His heart feels the ache and he is full of remorse. This kind of love is so deep that it is not possible to express it in words. The chamberlains describes this condition of Dushyanta as-

> "He loathes all beautiful things; to his ministers
> He is not free of access as before;
> He passes nights sleepless, tossing in bed;
> To the queens in the Royal Apartments,
> He extends all formal curtsies, but
> Addressing them wrongly, mistaking their names;
> Then, he remains long plunged in painfull embarrassment."[17]

The condition of Dushyanta becomes very bad as he madly remembers Shakuntala. In a similar manner we can find in Vipralambha Sringara of Vidyapati there is love in separation. Radha accepts that she cannot live without krishna. She feels lonely in the absence of her lover and it is a very painful experience in love. In Kalidasa this pain is heightened because Dushyanta understands his fault that he never cared for Shakuntala because of a curse. When Dushyanta gains back all of his memories associated with Shakuntala, he finds himself in a very traumatic condition. Thus we can say that when he knows about the reality of love between Shakuntala and himself the he becomes restless. He was living a very comfortable life when he was not aware about Shakuntala because of the effect of a curse. The knowledge of the realistic situation turns him restless and we can say that he got carried away from the realms of innocence to the world of experience. It is a very unusual feeling as he suddenly realizes all of his promises and responsibilities. In sonnet number one hundred and sixteen, Shakespeare has said that true love never changes with the change of time. It remains as constant as the Northern star, and thus, it acts as a guide to life. It means that it is very tough to find true love. If any feeling of love changes with the passage of time then it cannot be considered as a true love. Shakespeare was in love with his friend and his love remained always constant. If any beloved shifts her attention from her lover to some other men then it can be said that she is not a true beloved although the lover can be loyal or true to her. In such cases the loyalty of the beloved falls under question that what kind of relationship she is maintaining? The lover is true and loyal but he is cheated by his beloved. Such kind of relationship does not continue for a longer time as it is not constant. So in love both the lover as well as the beloved needs to be loyal to each other so that they can understand the value of life. It cannot be understood properly until we quote some lines from the poem-

> "Let me not to the marriage of true minds
> Admit impediments, love is not love
> Which alters when it alteration finds,
> Or bends with the remover to remove.
> O no, it is an ever-fixed mark
> That looks on tempests and is never shaken;
> It is the star to every wand'ring bark,
> Whose worth's unknown, although his height be taken...."[18]

If a lover is very far away from his beloved then there are possibilities that he will be in a painful condition. He must be remembering his beloved and scholars have said that the intensity of a love increases in any long distance relationship. For the beloved also it is equally applicable as we have seen this in the case of Radha. Vidyapati has beautifully presented the pain of Radha and she has also accepted that she cannot live happily without her lover. There are chances that in a long distance relationship the lover might search other women and the beloved too might have some other man but in such circumstances we cannot say that it is a kind of love. In such situations both the lover and the beloved are cheating themselves and they cannot feel the pain of love in separation because although they are separated but their needs are fulfilled through illegitimate affairs. Thus, this vipralambha Sringara which brings out pain in love can be treated as a checkpoint both for the lover as well as the beloved. In the English translated version of Vidyapati's work Sri Aurobindo says that-

> " If I leave thee, if I touch
> Other lady of delight,
> Let this snake my bosom bite
> If thou deem my error such
> Be thy malice on my spent
> In many an amorous punishment.
> Bind my body with thine arms,
> Scourge my limbs with pretty harms,..."[19]

Thus we can see that there is a kind of bond or promise between a lover and his beloved. Both of them are not supposed to break any bond of love. This bond or promise is tied by the knots of trust. So trust between a lover and his beloved acts like a pillar which gets stronger and stronger by the passage of time. Studying love traditions in Vidyapati and British Poets is a kind of honour as well as enjoyment mixed together. We have seen that understanding Vidyapati is not an easy task but when it comes to the topic like love it becomes very interesting. Love is a very basic emotion of life which is as easy to understand as complex is its nature. Reading love poetry and the existence of poets depends upon the society in which we live. Finally it can be said that the influence of Vidyapati can be seen on the young poets who love to write about love. In reality shows the songs of Vidyapati are sung today and it seems very fashionable. Singers find divinity and solace in the songs of Vidyapati. In comparison to British Poets Vidyapati stands very far ahead and I hope that one day the time will come when the world will accept his greatness.

NOTES AND REFERENCES

1. These lines have been taken from *Spectator* number 160 written by Addison. It was a daily publication which was founded by Addison and Steele in England from 1711 to 1712.
2. https://books.google.co.in/books?isbn=113949709X
3. It was a title given to Vidyapati by the vaishnav sects of Bengal for his devotional songs and love poems.
4. In Devi –Vandana Vidyapati invokes Goddess Durga. It must be taken into account that Devi Vandana is one of his most celebrated sect of writing poetry.
5. In Janaki- Vandana Vidyapati has written about Sita who is beautiful and submissive.
6. Jain, Manju, *Selected Poems and A Critical Reading of the Selected Poems of T.S.Eliot*, Oxford University Press, New Delhi, 2000, p.23
7. https://www.poetryfoundation.org/poems/43687/the-tyger
8. These are the lines 395 to 397 taken from *The Wasteland* written by T.S.Eliot.
9. Earlier Himalaya was known as Himavant.
10. Lines taken from *Childe Harold's Pilgrimage* written by Byron.
11. https://www.poets.org/poetsorg/poem/kubla-khan

12. Shiv –Vandana is the collection of poems mentioned in Padavali written by Vidyapati. Here the poet has tried to take the blessings of Lord Shiva.
13. https://en.wikipedia.org/wiki/Ardhanarishvara
14. Krishna-Vandana as the name suggests is a poem written for Shri Krishna. Vidyapati has written about the beauty and valour of Shri Krishna in this poem.
15. https://books.google.co.in/books?isbn=1351544535
16. Pranay –Prasang is the name of poems given by Vidyapati written on the subject of marriage and love. Here we can find amazing relationship between a lover and his beloved.
17. Jones, Sir William, Kalidasa's *Abhijnanasakuntalam*, Doaba Publications, New Delhi, 2005.p.45
18. www.shakespeare-online.com/sonnets/116detail.html
19. www.sriaurobindoashram.org/ashram/sriauro/downloadpdf.php?id=22

Bibliography

PRIMARY SOURCES

- Aldo S. Bernardo, *Petrarch, Laura and the Triumphs* (Albany: State U of New York P, 1974) p.8.

- Aldo, Petrarch, *Scipio and the "Africa"* (Baltimore: The Johns Hopkins P, 1962) p.68.

- Choudhary, Radha Krishna, *A Survey of Maithili Literature*, Shruti Publications,Delhi,1976,p.58

- Durling Robert M, *Petrarch's Lyric Poems* ,Cambridge university press, Harvard 1976.p.28

- Foster, Kenelm , *Petrarch Poet and Humanist* (University of Edinburgh press, Edinburgh , 1984.p. 25

- Gardner, J. *The Life and Times of Geoffrey Chaucer*, Vintage Books, New York, 1977.p.7

- Gardner, J. *The Life and Times of Geoffrey Chaucer*, Vintage Books, New York, 1977. P.18

- Hainsworth, Peter , *Petrarch The Poet*, Routledge publishers, New York, 1988 . p.122

- Jones, Sir William, Kalidasa's *Abhijnanasakuntalam*, Doaba Publications, New Delhi, 2005.p.45

- Muni, Bharta. *NatyaShastra*, Facsimile Publisher, Delhi, 2013. p.1

- Nicholas Kilmer, *Songs and Sonnets from Laura's Lifetime* (San Francisco: North Point P, 1981) xi

- Patterson, Lee *'Historical Criticism and the Development of Chaucer Studies'*, University of Wisconsin Press, 1987, Madison .p. 19

- Robert Giroux, *The Book Known As Q* (Saddle Brook, New Jersey: McClelland and Stewart Ltd., 1982) .p.31

- Sidney, Philip. *Astrophil and Stella*, Kessinger Publishing, Montana, 2010.p.5

- Whittock, T. *A Reading of The Canterbury Tales*, Cambridge University Press, Cambridge, 1968. p.115

SECONDARY SOURCES

- Abrams, M.H. *A Handbook of Literary Terms*, Wadsworth Cengage Learning, 2009, New Delhi. p. 226.

- Abrams, M.H.*A Handbook of Literary Terms*, Boston: Wadsworth, 2009.p.64

- An admirable account of Spenser's treatment of allegorical myths is given in C.S. Lewis's *The Allegory of Love*, Chapter 7

- *An Essay Concerning Human Understanding* by John Locke.

- Aurobindo, sri. *songs of Vidyapati*, Sri Aurobindo Ashram publishers, Pondicherry,1956,p.19

- Aurobindo, Sri. *Songs of Vidyapati*, Sri Aurobindo Ashram Publishers, Pondicherry,1956.p.5

- Baldesar, Castiglioni. *The Book of The Courtier*(New York: Penguin Books, 1978). p.338

- Baltimore, *Introduction to Image and Meaning Metaphoric Traditions in Renaissance Poetry*, 1960.p.7

- Blake, William. *The Four Zoas, Night The Second* in Poetry and prose, p.278

- Blake, William .*A Vision of the last Judgment*, The Nonesuch Press, London 1939.p.639.

- C.K. Ogden & I.A. Richards: The Meaning of Meaning, Trubner and Co. Ltd.London,1943.p9

- Duff, David. *Modern Genre Theory*. Harlow: Longman, United Kingdom, 2000. P.47

- E.K.Chambers & F. Sidgwick. *Early English Lyrics*, Sidgwick & Jackson publishers, London, 1937.p.1

- Eliot, T.S, Literary Essays of Ezra pound, Faber & Faber Press, London,1954.p.25

- Finneran, Richard J. (1996). The Collected Works of W.B. Yeats Volume I: The Poems: Revised Second Edition. Ed. New York: Scribner. p.77

- G.Wilson Knight. *The Wheel of Fire: Essays in Interpretation of Shakespeare's Sombre Tragedies*, 1930, Oxford University Press, London.p8.

- Gould, Eric. *Mythical Intentions in Modern Literature*. Princeton, N. J.: Princeton University Press, 1981. P.6

- Graham, Hough, *The Romantic Poets*, B.I. Publications, New Delhi, 1980.p.146
- Grierson, G.A. *The Test of A Man*, The Royal Asiatic Society, London, 1935.p.150
- Grierson, J.C. *Metaphysical Lyrics and Poems of the Seventeenth Century*, 1921,Clarendon Press, Oxford.p17.
- Hume, David. *A Treatise of Human Nature*. Edited by L. S. Selby-Bigge, 2nd ed. Revised by P.H. Nidditch. oxford: Clarendon Press, Oxford, 1978.
- Jain, Manju. *Selected Poems and A Critical Reading of the Selected Poems of T.S. Eliot*, Oxford University Press, New Delhi, 2000. p.23
- Kelly, John and Donville. Eric, *The Collected Letters of W. B. Yeats*, Vol. I, eds., Oxford: Clarendon Press.p.54
- Malaviya & Rizvi. *Donne and his Selected Poems*, Student Stores, Bareilly,1995.p.88
- *Milton's Verse, Scrutiny*, vol ii, September 1933. p.123
- Opacki, Ireneusz. *'Royal Genres.' Modern Genre Theory*. Ed. David Duff. Harlow: Longman, United Kingdom, 2000. P.119.
- Prasad,B. *An Introduction To English Criticism*, Macmillan India Ltd, New Delhi, 2007.p .2
- R.H.Robins: *General Linguistic*, Longman Publishers, London, 1971.p.371

- Sidney, Philip. An Apology for Poetry, Elizabethan critical essay, ed. G.Gregory Smith, London,1904.p.158

- Spurgeon ,Caroline. *Mysticism in English Literature*, 1913, Cambridge University Press,Cambridge.p2.

- *The Metaphysical Poets* p.273, it is also found in other critics like F.R. Leavis, in Imagery and Movement, *Scrutiny*, vol xiii

- Tillyard, E.M.W. *The Poetry of Sir Thomas Wyatt*, Chatto & Windus publishers, London,1949.p.6

- Williams, Oscar. *Master Poems of the English Language*, 1967, Washington Square Press, New York.p.370.

- Williamson, G. The Donne Tradition, Massachusetts,1930.p.48

SOURCES FROM THE INTERNET

- http://knarf.english.upenn.edu/Milton/pl9.html
- http://www.shakespeare-online.com/sonnets/130.html
- http://www.shakespeare-online.com/sonnets/3detail.html
- https://books.google.co.in/books?isbn=0199552096
- https://books.google.co.in/books?isbn=0691018618
- https://books.google.co.in/books?isbn=113949709X
- https://books.google.co.in/books?isbn=1351544535
- https://books.google.co.in/books?isbn=1400886252

- https://condor.depaul.edu/dsimpson/tlove/symposium.html
- https://en.wikipedia.org/wiki/Ardhanarishvara
- https://en.wikipedia.org/wiki/Piers_Plowman
- https://en.wikipedia.org/wiki/Platonic_love
- https://poemanalysis.com/ode-to-tomatoes-by-pablo-neruda-poem-analysis/
- https://www.aurobindo.ru/workings/sa/08/0155_e.htm
- https://www.poemhunter.com › Poems › Adonais
- https://www.poetryfoundation.org/.../astrophil-and-stella-1-loving-in-truth-and-fain-in...
- https://www.poetryfoundation.org/poems/43650/auguries-of-innocence
- https://www.poetryfoundation.org/poems/43687/the-tyger
- https://www.poetryfoundation.org/poems/43973/dejection-an-ode
- https://www.poetryfoundation.org/poems/44129/the-sun-rising
- https://www.poetryfoundation.org/poems/44688/to-his-coy-mistress
- https://www.poetryfoundation.org/poems/45190/amoretti-lxxix-men-call-you-fair
- https://www.poetryfoundation.org/poems/46467/the-flea
- https://www.poets.org/poetsorg/poem/kubla-khan

- https://www.theguardian.com/.../william-wordsworth-lines-composed-a-few-miles-abo.
- www.john-keats.com/gedichte/endymion_i.htm
- www.shakespeare-online.com/sonnets/116detail.html
- www.shakespeare-online.com/sonnets/130detail.html
- www.shakespeare-online.com/sonnets/18detail.html
- www.shakespeares-sonnets.com/sonnet/36
- www.sriaurobindoashram.org/ashram/sriauro/downloadpdf.php?id=22

✢✢✢✢✢✢✢✢

www.ingramcontent.com/pod-product-compliance
Lightning Source LLC
LaVergne TN
LVHW050028080526
838202LV00070B/6967